Advance Praise for *Finding Inner Courage*

"When Mark Nepo publishes a new book many, many readers rejoice. This time around, they have special reason to do so. *Finding Inner Courage* is perhaps Mark's finest book, a deep and graceful exploration of courage—the courage it takes to live life deep and live it whole—that will illumine your mind, strengthen your heart, and nourish your soul. May this book touch your life as it has touched mine. And may it help all of us live from that sacred core of selfhood that can heal us and our wounded world."
—Parker J. Palmer, author of *A Hidden Wholeness, Let Your Life Speak,* and *The Courage to Teach*

"What an extreme delight to be engaged with this writing that issues from the heart that thinks and the mind that poeticizes! How rare it is these days to find truly original writing and, even more, thought that has moved way, way beyond and beneath and above the kind of spectator consciousness that characterizes most writing. *Finding Inner Courage* is one of the handful of books I cherish."
—Robert Sardello, PhD, author of *Love and the World* and *Silence*

"Mark Nepo is a rare being, a poet who does not overuse language, a wise man without arrogance, a teacher who always speaks with compassion, and an easygoing love-to-listen-to-him storyteller. *Finding Inner Courage* is a collection of delicious essays. A feast for the spirit."
—James Fadiman, PhD, cofounder, Institute for Transpersonal Psychology

"Mark Nepo has the ability to provoke honest inquiry which simultaneously ignites reflection and motivates action. This is an invaluable book and resource for our changing times."
—Angeles Arrien, PhD, cultural anthropologist and author of *The Second Half of Life* and *The Four-Fold Way*

Also by Mark Nepo

Nonfiction: *As Far As the Heart Can See, Unlearning Back to God, The Exquisite Risk,* and *The Book of Awakening*

Poetry: *Surviving Has Made Me Crazy; Suite for the Living; Inhabiting Wonder; Acre of Light; Fire Without Witness;* and *God, the Maker of the Bed, and the Painter*

Editor: *Deepening the American Dream*

Recordings: *Inner Courage, Finding Our Way in the World,* and *Inside the Miracle*

FINDING INNER COURAGE

MARK NEPO
author of *The Book of Awakening*

Conari Press

First published in 2007 by Conari Press,
an imprint of Red Wheel/Weiser, LLC
With offices at:
665 Third Street, Suite 400
San Francisco, CA 94107
www.redwheelweiser.com

Permissions and copyright acknowledgments begin on p. 281.

ISBN: 978-1-57324-531-9
Library of Congress Cataloging-in-Publication Data available upon request.

Cover design by Jim Warner
Text design by Jessica Dacher
Typeset in Bembo and Priori
Cover photo © Carl Vilhelm Balsgaard/SuperStock, *Still Life of Oranges.*
Author photo by Brian Bankston (www.brianbankston.com)

Printed in the United States of America
TS
10 9 8 7 6 5 4 3 2 1

♻ Text paper contains a minimum of 50% post-consumer-waste material.

If your everyday practice is to open to all your emotions, to all the people you meet, to all the situations you encounter, without closing down, trusting that you can do that—then that will take you as far as you can go. And then you will understand all the teachings that anyone has ever taught.

✧ *Pema Chödrön*

Contents

To My Reader

The word *courage* comes from the Latin *cor*, which literally means *heart*. The original use of the word *courage* means *to stand by one's core*. This is a striking concept that reinforces the belief found in almost all traditions that living from the Center is what enables us to face whatever life has to offer. This book is an exploration into how to find our way to our core, to stand by our core, and to then sustain the practice of living from our core—to live out of our courage. To *encourage* means *to impart strength and confidence, to inspire and hearten*. So the questions unfold: How do we *encourage* ourselves, each other, and the world? And just what does it mean to live a life of *encouragement*?

If to find our way to our core is *to face the lion*, then to stand by our core is *to be the lion*. And to sustain the practice of living from our core—to live out of our courage—is to find our way in the world by tracking *inner courage and where it lives*. These notions frame the journey of this book.

Inner Courage and Outer Courage

The courage we all admire—where ordinary people summon unexpected strength to run into burning buildings or to stand up to tyrants, whether an abusive father or an abusive leader, this inspiring and mysterious impulse to rise and meet a dangerous situation, which Hemingway referred to as grace under pressure—grows from another kind of courage: inner courage. By inner courage, I mean the ground of quiet braveries from which the more visible braveries sprout. These are the ways of living and being that make bravery possible in the first place, not just as an event, but as an approach to life, as a way of life. This book is devoted to exploring those quiet braveries, in an effort to understand not only what constitutes courage in its deepest sense, but what is the soil in which it is seeded, watered, cared for, and grown.

Thinking about courage in this way opens us to an array of small and constant efforts that no one ever sees, but which have changed the world: the courage to feel, to see, to accept, to heal, to be. Efforts of this nature often go unnoticed and unrecognized. Like the courage to break life-draining patterns and let the story of our lives unfold. Like the courage to persevere through the doorway of nothing into the realm of everything. Like the courage to choose aliveness over woundedness, to remember what matters when we forget, and to build on the past instead of hiding in it. Like the courage to choose compassion over judgment and love over fear, to withstand the tension of opposites, and to give up what no longer works in order to stay close to what is sacred.

These subtle yet essential states, and more, make up the elements of living, and so it serves us well to explore how they grow singly and together. This is an education I never had in school, but which life has been shouting for as long as I can remember. This is an education of what matters.

What Does Courage Mean?

How we hold this question is important. It's interesting that the question, *what does it mean?* in Spanish, *que quiere decir?*, literally translates as, *what does it want to say?* The difference inherent in the Spanish view is that whatever holds meaning is alive and has its own vital authority and, therefore, demands us to be in relationship to it in order to learn its meaning. The English view readies us to *apprehend* meaning, while the Spanish view readies us to *experience* meaning. The Spanish view tells us that meaning can only be revealed by listening to the life waiting in the voice of every thing, and only by staying in relationship to that living voice will we experience meaning in our days.

So, when we ask *what does courage mean?* in Spanish, *Que quiere decir "courage"?*, it literally translates as, *what does courage want to say?* This is the question at the heart of this book. No doubt, courage will have something different to say to each of us. And like a friend who we each experience differently, our understanding of courage will live in the mysterious sum of all that we hear. In this way, this book is an invitation to begin a relationship with life itself, always listening for what it wants to say.

How to Read This Book

You will encounter many examples of courage in this book, many stories of ordinary people invoking the best of who they are in all kinds of moments, great and small. It is important how you relate to these stories. For it is easy to feel diminished rather than inspired by such remarkable events, so great is our urge to compare. But *inspire* means *to inhale*, not *measure against*. In truth, each of us is remarkable, and the little seed buried underground would blanch at the sight of its kind already in full bloom, never dreaming that such a magnificence would be possible in itself. Yet it is not only possible, but inevitable. It is the same with the potency of our souls. So I invite you to *inhale* these stories, to let them fill your lungs and circle your heart, to let them empower you to stand more firmly by your core and a little taller in the world.

I confess that I began writing this book looking to uncover and sustain my own courage. I confess that the part of me that is a poet is in awe, busy retrieving the aspects of the mystery that we are privileged to, while the part of me that is a philosopher is busy talking about what I find, always trying to understand what is retrieved. And the part of me that is a cancer survivor is always eager to turn mystery and understanding into food, to make use of it.

I have come to believe that we can only discover the capacity and meaning of our courage in the context of our struggles, in how we face and inhabit the challenges life presents to us. In this, courage is an applied art of spirit. It is not something we can manipulate, but only live into. Recovering the Source and living it out in the world, alone and together, is a lifelong devotion. One that we must, ultimately, inhabit alone, but one which we must enliven together.

Movement I

Facing the Lion

Wings of the Butterfly

If you bring out what is inside you,
what is inside you will save you.
If you fail to bring out what is inside you,
what is inside you will destroy you.

❖ *The Gnostic Gospels*

Somewhere in this time we live in, she was one of many, too
many, an orphan of war. Her story took place in Guatemala. Her
parents were killed and her brother lost in retaliation. And three
years later, this little girl, maybe nine or ten, was found pulling
the wings off a butterfly, muttering, *"Pobrecita . . . Pobrecita"*—
"Poor little one..."

The image has haunted me. For in her innocence and pain,
she revealed and relived the knot of our struggle as human beings: what we don't face as our own, we perpetrate on others.
I'm in no way blaming this little one. She was just a tiny angel
sent to remind us. But it has worked on me, the struggle she
enacted for us all. She, of course, was the poor little one whose
young wings had been torn. And carrying a pain too big for her
small heart, she was, I think, trying to alleviate her pain by acting
out her wound on something else. This, to me, is the source of
much of the pain we cause in this life.

It is not new either. As far back as 7,000 years ago in the land
of Sumeria, the tale of Gilgamesh was first told. It is the story

of an empty and sad king who is so detached from life that he seeks adventure and battle to know he is alive. Thus, he declares war on Humbaba, the forest deity, proclaiming he must be killed. Along the way, the story says that, "Like many before him, Gilgamesh sought to slay Humbaba rather than face the undiscovered country in himself."

Throughout time, the role of consciousness and compassion in our lives has been to help us face our own experience and demons, to face the undiscovered country in ourselves. Largely, so we won't hurt each other. Indeed, the original meaning of the Muslim word *jihad* is *to face one's own demons*. This is the holy war. Without the ability to face our own demons, we often seek revenge rather than feel what is ours to feel. For vengeance is a powerful distraction from accepting the legitimate suffering that arises from the wheel of life; an acceptance that can make kindred spirits of us all, if we let it.

And so I feel compelled to inquire into the art of facing things—facing ourselves, each other, and the unknown. It is something we cannot do without, for facing things is what courage, at its most fundamental level, is all about. Without this, we replay and pass our suffering on to others repeatedly.

Each of us is the little one with the torn heart and much— indeed, the world—depends on whether we tear each other's wings or face ourselves and each other with tenderness. Yet where do we find the honesty and resilience for that? We can begin by asking: How many of us suffer the trauma of thinking that life is a tearing of wings? And what do we do in our quiet terror to avoid being torn? In these small questions, the most meaningful courage can grow until, against all odds, against the legacies of being torn, we might be able to stop hiding and pretending. Only then can we discover directly, for ourselves, what constitutes survival. For every time we face our own pain at being broken, we dissolve the heart's need to relive the break.

The Undiscovered Country

Let us present the same face to everyone.

❖ *Lao Tzu*

The cultural anthropologist Angeles Arrien has discovered that every indigenous culture on earth shares a common description of the cycle of experience. Though stated and honored in many ways, that central wisdom essentially says: *what is not integrated is repeated.* Just what does this mean? It doesn't mean that any of us are exempt from pain or chancing into the territory of injustice. It doesn't mean that we will not see things break down or fall apart. What it does mean is that whether pain and suffering will have a proper place in our lives or whether we will be trapped in the canyon of pain and suffering depends on our efforts to integrate our experience into a wholeness that then releases its wisdom.

It is a law of the journey: *what is not integrated is repeated.* What we won't face or express moves into our hands as a compulsion to speak itself through our actions: that little Guatamalan girl forcing the rip in her heart onto the small butterfly; my pain at being rejected by one friend being played out unconsciously on another; a sad and empty teacher painting a sad and empty world for his students; or a doctor pushed and abused in medical school pushing and abusing his patients years later. You can fill in the unconscious equation any way you like. Inevitably, what we won't face or express moves through our hands into the world.

You can see that we always have a choice between the effort to integrate, to surface and join what life brings to us, or to hide and disintegrate what life brings our way. For the opposite of joining is not just static. It becomes destructive. In describing his sadness at not being able to help a friend, the sociologist Jean Vanier remarks, "He had not come to terms with his own brokenness; all this was still hidden in the tomb of his being." Vanier goes on to say that instead of integrating the place of brokenness within him, his friend grew to see the world as broken. Not facing his own wounds led to a greater brokenness that was even more difficult to escape.

To state the case plainly, there is rarely a neutral place in between. Those who are not busy trying to integrate are busy disintegrating. So we don't have the luxury of sitting this one out! Still, the courage to be conscious and caring alone will mitigate our suffering. For the courage to lean into what needs to be joined, instead of hiding from it, will keep our brokenness from spreading. A recurring theme of wakefulness is that facing, feeling, and accepting our own suffering keeps us from reenacting it on others. Facing the undiscovered country in ourselves often stops the bleeding. It often stops the disintegration. Thus, a central goal of inner courage is to bear our humanness and integrate our experience so that we might strengthen the bond between living things and not add to the tearing of wings smaller than our own.

Vengeance or Music

When pushed below our
frightened sense of self,
we do not die. We live.

History has shown that if we don't find the courage to face our own experience, that unconscious spiral can lead to vengeance. If unchecked, it can fester into a deeper form of violence that we call evil.

The renowned psychiatrist Gerald May describes vengeance as a diversion from the hard work of facing our own suffering. Even children experience this diversion of vengeance:

Years later, I learned of some studies of traumatized children in which an attitude of revenge seemed to compensate for what otherwise would have been paralyzing depression. At last I began to see how, at a primitive psychological level, vengeance [can] serve a certain self-protective function. It by no means prevents future injury, but it [can] function as a defense against the reality of insults or injuries that have already been sustained. In the absence of revenge, we would be left with the bare pain of our loss, the sheer awful fact of it. Without revenge, we would have to bear what may seem like bottomless grief and despair. We would have to see ourselves.

While these insights make the gears of vengeance visible, they don't justify it. May simply and strongly shows how difficult it is for us to bare our own pain and loss. Often, it is an unconscious sequence of little choices—to hide instead of face, to lie instead of cry, to harden instead of staying vulnerable—that leads us to a numb place where we can't recognize ourselves. The writer and director Menno Meyjes speaks to this human struggle with little choices as his impetus to create the film *Max* (2002), which focuses on the development of Adolf Hitler's aberrance as a human being:

The movie isn't about Hitler's great crimes. The audience knows all about them already. This is about his small sins—his emotional cowardice, his relentless self-pity, his envy, his frustration, the way he collects and nurtures offenses—because those are the sins we can see when we look in a mirror.

Hitler, like Osama and Saddam and Milosevic, obliges us by representing an uncomplicated picture of evil. But nobody wakes up one day and slaughters thousands. They make choices, one at a time, and they do it because they do not have the courage . . . to give up illusions and look within and accept one's humanity.

What Menno Meyjes raises here is very profound and challenging for every human being. For it is the simple, daily choices—or lack of choices—that enable power over compassion and self-righteousness over empathy. Countless times in our days, we find ourselves faced with the almost imperceptible choice to enable trust or distrust, to affirm directness or indirectness, to empower anonymous judgment or the courage to stand in one's truth without judging others. In minute ways, each time we let distrust, indirectness, and anonymous judgment spread and deepen between us, we water the seeds of evil that make a Hitler or Milosevic possible. I cannot overstate this connection. If a butterfly beating its wings in China can cause a strong wind on the other side of the world, then the seeds of inhumanity that we all carry, the small wings we tear in private, can incubate darkly over a continent of time into something horrific. It is all connected, and all our choices contribute to what appears before us: love or hate, welcome or disdain, compassion or cruelty.

Other traditions speak, as well, to these ethical forks in the road. The philosopher Jacob Needleman speaks of the ancient Greek notion of *Thumos*, which means *spirit of fight*. The Greeks believed this to be a part of human nature. Whether it becomes a destructive or healing energy in the world depends largely on whether that spirit of fight or struggle is directed in self-centered ways at the disappointments we experience in not getting what we want, or in deeper, self-transforming ways that seek out the resources of spirit, love, and truth. It seems to be perennially true that if that spirit of fight or struggle is not directed at what distances us from God (our isolations and illusions), then it will be directed at others. Needleman suggests that the misdirection of *Thumos*, our spirit of fight or struggle, has been a timeless source of war, evil, and unnecessary woundedness in the world.

Yet when we can find and stand by our core, when we can face our isolations and illusions directly, we have the chance to enliven a different kind of relationship with the pain of life. To understand this, we need to consider the nature of a flute. It is a simple fact that a flute cannot make any music if it has no holes for the breath of life to pass through. Each being on earth is such a flute, and each of us releases our unique song of spirit through the holes carved by our experience through the years. Like it or not, this is one of the purposes of suffering.

And since no two flutes have the same holes carved in them, no two flutes make the same music. Likewise, no two beings sing the same song, since the holes in each life produce their own unrepeatable melody. All this to say that there is a great, ongoing choice that awaits us every day: whether we go around carving holes in others because we have been so painfully carved ourselves, or whether we let spirit play its song through our tender experience, enabling us to listen, as well, to the miraculous music coming through others. When experience opens us and spirit moves through, we can be astonished into humility. Once opened in this way, there is great strength and joy in listening together for the song of spirit that arises so uniquely from our brush with life on earth. In submitting to this journey, courage can turn wounds into openings. In embracing this journey, love can turn brokenness into song.

Wrestling with God

Like an inlet worn open
by unceasing depths,
I can no longer decide
what belongs in or out.

This ever-present choice—between facing our own experience
or perpetrating it on others, between integrating or disintegrating, between empowering vengeance or enlivening the music of
spirit—requires another kind of spiritual practice that wrestles
to keep our inner and outer lives aligned and congruent. The
ongoing struggle between these energies is, in some fundamental way, what we are put here for. Waking in the midst of these
choices evokes an engaged practice of living that makes use of
both being and doing. It is both receptive and active.

The Jewish tradition speaks to this ongoing engagement with
experience as a necessary form of wrestling with God. The assumption under this sort of practice is that head-on engagement
and heart-on engagement with the mysteries of life hone us to
what is essential. It is a courageous engagement that wears away
whatever is extraneous. Repeatedly, our vitality often comes
alive from our wrestling with the energies of God.

This form of give and take is beautifully described in the Old
Testament story of Jacob, when he "plunged down into the profound ravine of the Jabbok thousands of feet below." Reaching

the strong river rushing at the bottom, he found the place of crossing and sent his family and all his belongings on. There he waited, not sure for what, until an apparition appeared and wrestled with him all through the night. At the sign of first light, the figure went to flee, but Jacob held on saying, "I will not let thee go, except thou bless me." Finally, the spirit gave Jacob its blessing and vanished as dawn flooded the length of the river. The spirit refused to name itself, but Jacob knew he'd seen the face of God. From that point on, Jacob was known as *Israel*, which is Hebrew for *God-Wrestler*.

The essence of Jacob's journey awaits anyone who dares to search for God and who thinks truth might have something to do with it. For who among us, in our heart of hearts, can deny that such a profound ravine exists within us all, waiting for the instant we summon the courage to descend into our own depths? And, against all our fears, at the base of this profound ravine is that portion of God's river cutting through our deepest stone.

The story seems to say: if you can descend to your rock bottom, no matter what brings you there, you will find God's river. And, at the place of crossing, if you put down all that you carry, if you send on all that you love, if naked of all attachment you wait in your deepest rock through your darkest night, the spirit of the Universe will enfold you, and you will have the chance of a lifetime to turn and bend, to wrestle with the elusive Being of the World. Then, if you can hold on until there is a trace of fresh light, the ineffable will reveal itself to you, and that revelation will bless you, renew you, enable you to wade through God's river into the freshness of original living.

This is a parable of transformation worth meditating on. I invite you to retell it while personalizing all the players: placing yourself as Jacob, naming your loved ones who travel with you, particularizing the landscape of your own ravine, describing the taste of God's stream that you alone know, and putting a face and voice on the spirit that you wrestle with. Imagine your conversation with that spirit. Enter the parable again with all these personal faces and see what you learn.

At the heart of it, the story confirms that at the bottom of our toughest troubles flows God's stream. It tells us that by facing our own experience there, we will be forced into a baptism that confronts our deepest assumptions about life. It is important to note that in facing these things and wrestling with God, the purpose is not to conquer or pin God, but to take hold of what is essential and elusive at the heart of our experience and stay in embrace with it until it reveals its secrets and blesses our journey. Inevitably, we are given the chance, again and again, to face the river at the bottom of our ravine, where we will rise either more committed to seeking vengeance in a life of wounds or to making music out of our suffering.

Just what happens in that ravine, to be honest, is hard to say. I can only speak from my own experience. Entering that ravine does not seem to be something that we can will, or set up, or orchestrate. But when we're wounded, we have a chance to enter the ravine of that wound. When our sense of things is undone, we have a chance to enter the ravine of our confusion. When we are thrust into loss and grief, we have the sorry chance to descend into the ravine of that awful loss or grief. I know, for me, in those moments when I have been able to face the travails that life has presented me, sometimes there is a glimpse of a spirit or angel that I can hold onto. And in that moment of hold, I have been able to love the part of me that is hurt, the part of the world that is ugly, and the dark side of God's face that is so difficult to understand. And briefly—when I have wrestled with the wounds of my cancer, with the loss of loved ones and friends, with the end of a long marriage, with the pain of innocents slaughtered in the machine of time halfway around the world—I somehow can rise loving all of life more, all of the mystery more, all of our human flaws more, all of my peculiar stumblings even more. Though I can't say how, I can bear witness that each wound is a threshold into God's ravine in which our nameless angel waits.

In psychological terms, the moment of divine hold at the base of who we are is a terrifying one in which all that is unnamable by its very nature remains elusive, changing shape over and over. Because of this, when we, finally in the chasm of our own life, in our darkest night, hold onto the Being of the World, we hold a writhing mirror of ourselves that turns from lion to serpent to worm. This effort to face ourselves can rearrange who we are. In this moment, if we can hold to our darkest elements—in fact, embrace them—we might become whole. Nothing is harder than to enter our own depths and embrace the underside of our own nature, to say to our shadow-self as it flails in our arms, "I will not let thee go, except thou bless me."

These changing appearances that elude our grip, these shifting forms of life energy, are the many faces of God. And since the beginning of time, the essential seed in us, our soul, has always been ready to love-wrestle the Divine for its gifts—for glimpses of wholeness, for moments of insight and inexplicable love, for seeds of transformation. These are all gifts that cannot be possessed or owned lest they vanish. They can only be faced and embraced. As the great Taoist master Lao Tzu says, having without possessing is part of the supreme virtue. The things that matter most can be touched but not forced to linger. For trying to hold onto our pain or our joy is like trying to hold a wave even as it douses you. In actuality, we all must deal with the fleeting, perennial task of spiritual turning or bending, of love-wrestling from God's Being the very life force that we chase and resist during the tumble of our days.

Paradoxically, we are asked to both refresh and mature our innocence at the same time. By maturity, I do not mean the sullen and cynical acceptance of the broken side of things as the dominant shaper of the world. Rather, a more balanced acceptance of the cycle of experience on earth that is always forming and breaking down and forming anew. An acceptance that we are not exempt from that mysterious process and that only by facing and love-wrestling with the face of God that speaks to us can we survive the broken side of things.

When I think of the little Guatemalan girl tearing the wings off her butterfly, I can see the tiny broken angel inside me, waiting, if not held, to tear something smaller. This possibility is never far. But the other side is always near, too, as wonderfully evoked in this poem by a fourth grader in Detroit, Michigan, Cameron Penny:

If you are lucky in this life,
a window will appear between two armies on a battlefield.
Instead of seeing their enemies in the window, the soldiers
see themselves as children. They stop fighting and go home
and sleep. When they wake up, the land is well again.

Letting the Story Unfold

There are pearls in the deep sea, but one must hazard all to find
them. If diving once does not bring you pearls, you need not
conclude that the sea is without them. Dive again and again.

❖ Ramakrishna

In many regards, time is a path that, if allowed to unfold, will
lead us right into the heart of what matters. In real terms, we
need to trust time. This can be very difficult as we all fear death,
which waits at the end of our time. This fear, unchecked, leads
us to anticipate that the unexpected will be catastrophic, when
in truth it can just as often be bountiful and refreshing. In the
face of this, a life well lived can be understood as one that risks
not being trapped or governed by its fears, one that follows the
pulse of what matters as it presents itself. This is not to say that
we will ever be free of fear, but that, in spite of our fear, we can
be drawn by what matters down the unplanned path of time,
where we are often called to choose what is actually there over
what we thought we'd find. In day-to-day terms, to let time unfold tests our courage. It asks us repeatedly to stand by our core
and unlock our fear and let the story we are in continue, so that
we might live closer to the elemental moment that is constantly
forming everything.

A great story of time unfolding is how flowers, after the ice age, migrated from China to repollinate the world. Once covered with vegetation of all kinds, the earth was blanketed by ice and, during that time, almost everything living was frozen and buried. For a seemingly endless spell, we were an ice-covered planet spinning in space, just drifting there like the heart of a god gone numb from all the pain the living have inflicted on each other. It must have seemed that life on earth was at an end. But the glaciers failed to cover one vastness known to us as China.

There, though it was difficult, flowers and trees kept inching their way until they broke surface. Eventually, as the story of the earth's thawing slowly unfolded, the glaciers receded. And, over centuries, the winds blew pollen in every direction, and animals started to appear again, carrying seeds and thistles unknowingly on their fur. Then tribes began to migrate, repopulating the earth. Some brought flowers with them. Some didn't know what was carried on their coats. Finally, others came to China and, marveling at peonies and tulips and orchids, they brought flowers back to England, and soon Europe was in spring.

This slow reseeding of the earth is a metaphor for how we grow. For sometimes we are frozen and buried. Sometimes it seems that life is at an end. But if we can let the story we are in unfold, then the mystery of time will keep moving through us, and we will be returned to the heart of what matters. Often this is what happens when we lose someone we love. The earth seems to freeze over and life stalls. But eventually, even against the sanctity of our grief, the glacier around our heart begins to thaw, and we start to pick up seeds that, in spite of our pain, start to grow. And then, one summer day, when a small bird sings in our ear, we turn and in the sunlit window we see the reflection of a flower blooming inside our pain.

The truth is that, given enough time, life bestows its gifts, a drop at a time, if we can find the courage to stay open to the mysterious flow that is larger than any one event.

The Boy and the Drum

How little I have for coming
all this way, just my heart
that whips like a flag.

There is an old Hindu story. In it, there is a boy who wants a drum, but his mother can't afford a drum, and so, sadly, she gives him a stick. Though he doesn't know what to do with it, he shuffles home and begins to play with the stick. Just then, he encounters an old woman trying to light her *chulha*, her woodstove. The boy freely gives her the stick. She lights her fire, makes some bread, and in return she gives him half a loaf. Walking on, the boy comes upon a potter's wife whose child is crying from hunger. The boy freely gives her the bread. In gratitude, she gives him a pot. Though he doesn't know what to do with it, he carries it along the river, where he sees a washerman and his wife quarreling because the wife broke their one pot. The boy gives them the pot. In return, they give him a coat. Since the boy isn't cold, he carries the coat until he comes to a bridge, where a man is shivering. Riding to town on a horse, the man was attacked and robbed of everything but his horse. The boy freely gives him the coat. Humbled, the man gives him his horse. Not knowing how to ride, the boy walks the horse into town, where he meets a wedding party with musicians. The bridegroom and his family are all sitting under a tree with long faces. According to custom, the bridegroom is to enter the procession on a horse, which hasn't shown up. The boy freely gives him the horse. Relieved, the bridegroom asks what he can do for the boy. Seeing the drummer surrounded by all his drums, the boy asks for the smallest drum, which the musician gladly gives him.

This story serves as a good example that, underneath our trouble, the true nature of generosity is only fully visible if we let the story—whatever it is—unfold. If we limit the old teaching story to the boy asking for one thing and his mother bringing him another, we have a lesson in not getting what we want, but accepting what we are given. If we end the story when the boy gives the woman the stick, we have a moment of altruism or sacrifice, depending on how we look at it. If we end the story when the woman gives the boy half a loaf of bread, it becomes a lesson in barter and fair exchange, trading what's timely and of use. But if we let the story take its full and natural course, we are given something quite different. For the longer we let relationships unfold, the more we see how everything goes together and how answering the needs of others depends on how we accept what we're given as unexpected medicine, even if it's not what we want.

Often, this courage—to wait and let the fabric of the Universe reveal itself—dissolves our individual sense of ownership into a sense of guardianship over gifts that no one owns. In this larger fabric, gifts rush through the Universe, moving from one place of need to another in a pattern too big to really see, in much the same way that blood rushes to a place of injury in the body. This humble story, allowed to unfold, lets us recognize that the unexpected gift that comes our way might not be for us. It might be that, like the Hindu boy, we are called to carry it to another. We might be but one exchange along the way and one exchange from realizing how we are all connected.

The Power of Passing Through So Many Hands

By assuming that we alone author and own the gifts that we give, and by limiting our acts of giving to a surface understanding of one exchange, we often lose the deeper meaning that true generosity awakens. Sadly, viewing others from our smaller frame of reference cuts us off from resources and wisdom. This limited way of seeing ultimately rejects any idea or person that is not like us. A powerful example is how Westerners have misconstrued the Native American understanding of what it means to give. We've all heard the term "Indian giver" and its Western meaning that denigrates someone who gives something and then asks for it back. In our unwillingness to let the story unfold, we miss the beautiful and profound truth of how Native Americans give and receive, which presumes that no one owns the gift. Rather, it is understood in Native American culture that the gift is to flow, to be passed back and forth to whoever needs it most. In this way, the gift mysteriously gains sanctity and power for passing through so many hands, including even those who offered it in the first place.

It reminds me of a relic of a saint someone gave me when I had cancer, a chip of bone from someone centuries ago who began a religion I was not a part of. As I held onto the relic, I worried and prayed and kept sweating through my terror. The relic became precious to me. Once well, it became a sacred aid for me, until one day the person who gave it to me fell terribly ill and needed it back. Was she an "Indian giver" in the Western misnaming? Hardly. Were we beautifully thrown into the mysterious sanctity of the gift gaining power as it moved back and forth between us? Amazingly so. I was afraid to give the relic up and felt naked without it, but giving it up made everything holy. I have since, when the time proved right, given away other precious things I have lived with, treasures I have carried for years, belongings I have long held dear. For I have learned that only in use does the gift continue to heal.

In the case of the boy and the drum, the smaller, truncated stories within the larger story show us how people give to each other in times of need. But the larger version of the story shows us how staying in relationship and staying open to a continual practice of giving and receiving opens the mystery of abundance that informs all circumstance, even when we feel blinded by our need.

Still, this courage to return to a larger view is easy to forget and hard to take hold of. Because of that, and because of its importance in restoring our sense of being a part of something larger than ourselves, this return to a larger view is a central task of education; an education that helps us face life and live in the world. It always helps to let the story unfold from seven exchanges to seven generations, and beyond if necessary. In the unfolding is the way.

The Swan and the Tailor

From God's eye, there are no
countries, no policies, no visas.
There is only one earth softened
by one sweet water.

There are two very different but wonderful examples of how
following our questions can lead us into a deeper way of living.
By letting the story before them draw them further and further
into it, both the Hindu spiritual leader Ramakrishna and the
American Quaker John Woolman discovered a fountainhead of
truth.

For the first story, we need to go back to nineteenth-cen-
tury India when the British Empire was at its height. There, in
the northeastern part of that magnificent subcontinent, in the
province of Bengal, a spiritual leader was born. It was three years
after the death of India's first Universalist, Rammohun. It is said
that when the Atman of many unborn beings gathered to enter
life through the birth of Ramakrishna, the tigers looked up from
the tall grasses, feeling a wind that wasn't there. No one could
know that Ramakrishna (1836–1886) would take Rammohun's
understanding of the common center of all spiritual paths to
another level of experience. Little did anyone know that the
journey of Ramakrishna would become legend. No one could
know that Ramakrishna would follow his want for the Divine

beyond the boundaries of his own Hindu tradition, and that he would bravely and simply live the many traditions to their common center.

In his childhood, it became clear that his capacity to be touched by essence was extraordinary. It is told that, as a small child, he happened one evening upon a flock of snow white cranes and chanced to watch them pierce a darkening cloud. The flight of these birds parting the dark sent him into such a trance that he lost consciousness and had to be carried home by some villagers who found him lying on the side of the road. Those close to him knew that this enormous sensitivity was a sign that his spirit lived at the Center and could not be named.

Later, at the age of twenty, Ramakrishna would submit himself for twelve years to many gurus and many practices, including Hindu, Christian, and Muslim devotions. After this arduous journey, he would declare, out of his own direct experience, that each path led him to illumination, that any holy way could bring a single being into the ultimate reality, if their surrender to God was sufficiently intense. As his legend grew, the people began to call him *Paramahamsa*, the supreme swan.

What is inspiring about this sage is that he let his quest for sacredness unfold beyond what he was taught. And, along the way, he was able to witness, from his own firsthand experience, that all spiritual paths work. Each can lead a human being to the realization of God. More than the particular devotions Ramakrishna tried, it was his sincere curiosity about the sacred that enabled him to follow his questions and to surrender to the experience of spiritual paths other than his own. In his sincerity, Ramakrishna quietly made visible a courage that allowed him to drink from the illumined lake from which all saints drink. Following the-story-he-was-awakened-into led him into the heart of what is sacred. He came away with experiential proof of the unity of all religions. His small room in the Dakshineswar temple garden on the outskirts of Calcutta became an oasis for all seekers, even atheists. His great contribution was that he saw God and unity in all.

For our second story, we need to go back a hundred years before the birth of the supreme swan to pre-revolutionary America. There we find John Woolman (1720–1772), the tailor from colonial New Jersey who abolished slavery within the Quaker community almost eighty years before the Civil War. I am indebted to Parker Palmer for bringing me to the life of John Woolman. For a more in-depth look into the moral example of John Woolman and his Quaker community, there is no better guide than Parker's exceptional essay, "The Politics of the Broken-Hearted: On Holding the Tensions of Democracy." He tells Woolman's story so well that I'll share his words with you here:

A tailor by trade, Woolman lived among Quaker farmers and merchants whose religious beliefs held all human beings as equal in the eyes of God but whose affluence depended heavily on slave labor. He received "a revelation from God" that slavery was an abomination and that Quakers should set their slaves free. For twenty years, at great personal cost, Woolman devoted himself to sharing this revelation with members of his religious community, "walking his talk" with every step. When he visited a remote farmhouse to share his revelation, he would fast rather than eat a meal prepared or served by slaves. If he inadvertently benefited from a slave's labor, he would insist on paying that person.

Woolman quietly and persistently carried a spiritual courage within him wherever he went. Without forcing his views on anyone, he carried his question about slavery like a lantern that he held before all that he met, and that light, slowly but surely, illumined the dark corners of their minds. It is interesting to understand how the American Quaker community dealt with slavery in contrast to how the rest of America did.

When Woolman first brought his question about slavery to his own Quaker circle, they took the question very seriously, reflecting on it and discussing it at length. Still, they could not come to consensus. But here's the unprecedented lesson. Instead of shutting down the minority view, instead of censuring or even exiling Woolman as a pariah, his Quaker circle said that though they could not agree with him, they could see that he had been touched by something sacred in this. And so they invited him to pursue this question among the rest of their Quaker circles across America. If he would do this, they would provide for his family, Woolman accepted their charge, and they awaited the findings of his journey.

As he traveled by foot, word spread about the quiet Quaker with the deep presence. When speaking without a translator to a Native American elder, the leader, moved by Woolman's sheer presence, came over, placed his hand on Woolman's chest and said, "I like to feel where words come from." Not knowing what the elder had said, Woolman placed his hand on the elder's chest and simply bowed.

No one knew that this journey would take Woolman close to twenty years, as he walked through almost every Quaker community along the East Coast, following his question about the rightness of slavery into home after home, opening conversation after conversation, and listening to the story of his community unfold, an exchange at a time. The result was as extraordinary as it was quiet. Finally, the Quaker community in America arrived at a consensus to free all their slaves. And, in 1783, eleven years after John Woolman's death, the Quaker community as a whole petitioned Congress to correct the "complicated evils" of slavery.

If John Woolman had never had the courage to follow his deepest questions, the Quaker story of ending slavery would have never unfolded. If his community had seen only Woolman's opinions and not his devotion of heart, they would have never encouraged his journey or supported his family. His story is a remarkable example of individual and collective courage. In retrospect, it is instructive and troubling that the Quaker example was completely ignored. Instead, the rest of America solved the issue of slavery, almost three generations later, by perpetrating on itself one of the bloodiest wars in modern history.

These are extraordinary examples of inner courage whose glare might distract us, as when we look directly into the sun. Rather let's look at what such courage sheds light on. Which means, what can we take from the swan and the tailor that can be applied to our own lives? For each of us, in our own way, are on personal quests for a direct experience of what is sacred and for a direct experience of true community. Just what then did Ramakrishna and John Woolman have in common?

Well, both had a tireless courage in how they listened. Like a Native American standing still in the woods until he can hear a worm moving beneath the leaves, both stood still in the forest of life until they could hear the pulse of what is sacred moving beneath the preconceptions and prejudices that generations had covered it with. Further, both had the courage to then trust and follow the bit of truth they heard, and what they heard created questions. They trusted that following their questions would lead them to a more truthful way of living. Then both had the courage to not hide what they heard or what they were called to follow. They neither imposed their sense on others, nor were they dissuaded to hide their own truth. Finally, these basic, timeless gestures of listening for what is sacred, trusting what you hear, and following where that leads, without imposing it on others and without hiding what you know—all these enabled them to let a deeper story of life unfold. This unfolding allowed both of them to find their destiny as realized beings, which, in turn, impacted the people they were blessed to travel with.

Our path may not be as dramatic, but our steps are the same. From seven exchanges to seven generations, the health of our relationships and our chance to know what is sacred often depend on whether we can enact these timeless gestures in our daily lives. Can we find the courage to listen and to follow our questions? Can we find the swan and the tailor within us? That is, can we find the part of our soul that will swim the one water of God and not claim it for any one shore? And can we find the part of our soul that will stitch the cloth that binds us all? And further, can we accept the swan and tailor in others?

Loving What You Fear

Go outside and let the sun spill into your heart.
There. Can you feel it? It's the quiver of your soul.
It makes you vulnerable but it will never betray you.

Sometimes the courage of others can be intimidating. Let me share a more ordinary example that involves my own struggle with fear. When barely a year old, I was set down to play at a neighbor's house while my parents had coffee. Thinking it cute, someone placed me on the back of a Dalmation. Everyone oohed and aahed, as I seemed a cowboy out of control riding his spotted horse. I have no memory of this, of course, but the story goes that the Dugan's man with his tray of donuts rang the doorbell, which frightened the dog, and I was flipped and scratched and bitten.

As far back as I can remember, I had a fear of dogs. I developed an added sense. I could hear the jingle of a collar a block away, could sense behind which trash can or shrub a stray dog was nosing about. I walked the suburban streets on guard, zigzagging from sidewalk to sidewalk, from corner to corner, even cutting across yards to avoid the Great Dane that the Olsons said was well trained.

Of course, dogs were everywhere, and I felt like I was carrying a terrible secret, a shameful weakness that I couldn't control, which I wanted no one to know, least of all young dog owners.

My parents urged me with exasperation not to show my fear, as if I was a slow and stubborn learner. "Once they know you're afraid, you're done for," my father would say. Only later on, after divorce and surgery, only when living three hundred miles from where I grew up, did I realize how much this curt little maxim said about his life.

When I was fourteen, a German shepherd chased me up a street pole, the kind that held those Monopoly-like street signs. There, atop a slender white sign that said "Massachusetts Ave.," I squatted as this police dog barked and jumped for my heels. People passed and pointed and laughed, but no one stopped to help. It's a funny scene now, but at the time I was humiliated and terrified. I stayed there till the dog grew tired and bored and left. I stayed for at least fifteen minutes afterward to make sure the dog was gone. When my feet hit the ground, I felt rubbery and nauseous, too embarrassed to run and too scared to walk, so I ran stiffly through the dull suburban streets back to my house. My parents seemed to find the whole thing amusing, and my father reiterated, as if impatient with a boy too dumb to master his bike, "You can't let them know you're afraid."

When I first went to college, there were stray dogs everywhere, and I had to confide in a few close friends to help me through. Changing my route at a second's notice, especially when walking by myself, became a common occurrence. The streets never felt free.

As I began teaching, I discovered an interesting parameter to my fear. The more secure I was feeling in my life, the smaller my sense of fear. The more uncentered and confused I was, the greater my sense of fear. The range of what I found fearful had much to do with my mood of confidence and clarity. In a palpable way, it was like having a ring of fear that encircled me. When I was muddled, the ring extended as far as a city block. When I was clear and calm, the ring retracted to only a few feet. At my best, I could be in a room with a calm dog, as long as the dog was below eye level and I wasn't sitting.

It was seven years later that I was stricken with cancer. It was a hellish journey through three years of surgeries and treatments that skinned me of many things, a tunnel of days upon days where I learned to face my fears and accept my own pain.

During that time, I went to the island of St. Martin, and it was there—in the lazy French streets of the rural seaport of Marigot—that I began to question my fear of dogs. Where did it really come from? Though I knew the story of the Dalmation, I couldn't remember it. I was walking down a street in Marigot after lunch one beautifully hot afternoon, and there were three dogs sleeping across the sidewalk. As I went to cross the street, I suddenly stopped and thought, why don't I see what happens? I wondered briefly if I had become so adept at honoring my reflex of fear that I was taking precautions before actually feeling afraid. I wondered if I allowed myself to get close, would I actually be afraid at all? Clearly, this was all possible because, after having cancer and facing death, the presence of a dog didn't seem to loom the way it always had. So I stepped slowly over the sleeping dogs, and I felt nothing—no fear, no tension—and the dogs didn't even stir. This was the beginning of a liberation.

The next Christmas, my loved ones took me for a ride, over two hours, to a farm in the middle of upstate New York. I had no idea what we were doing until we pulled into this long dirt road that led to a trailer and two full-grown golden retrievers were running to our car. I weakly protested, wasn't sure I could even get out of the car, but did. Once inside the trailer, I found a litter of eleven pups no more than four weeks old.

Before I knew it, I was on the trailer floor, pups climbing my lap, their tiny paws pressing against my legs and arms. And one—the largest female of the bunch, the quietest of the batch, the lightest of them all—kept coming back to me. In that instant on the trailer floor, against all my experience, I felt the rise of a moment that seemed like it would never appear again. I said, "I'll take her." I heard myself and felt excited and scared and crazy. But I said yes.

The breeder marked her tail with a blue Magic Marker. I named her Saba, for the mystical island south of St. Martin jutting so clearly from the ocean. When I brought her home, she slept the whole way in my coat, breathing warmly against my heart. And from the beginning, my want to love her began to dissipate my fear. For the first few weeks, she couldn't climb stairs, and so, like a new father, I carried her in and out, teaching her to pee. In the mornings, I'd sit on the kitchen floor, and she'd lie on my legs, belly up, licking my hands profusely.

Saba was only nine weeks old when my old friend Paul and I took her with us to a farm in Easton, New York. It was January. I'd only had her two weeks. She was about twelve pounds. After fixing some pipes in the cellar, we went for a walk by the grove of birch trees. Everything was covered with snow, and the stream was iced over except in the center. It was the first time Saba had run loose, her first winter, and she was ecstatic, sniffing and plowing through every branch and drift. Paul was trying to get a photo of the stream and the sunlit patterns of ice when Saba came barreling down the snow-covered slope. Unable to stop, she slid, her paws sputtering in reverse, right into the middle of the iced-over stream. In a second, I saw her small furry head arch up but not enough to break surface. In another second, without any thought at all, I was in the stream, up to my waist in ice water, scooping her up and tossing her over my shoulder. I saw her drift through the air and heard her land with a wet thud about ten feet from the stream. I climbed out, sopping, my wallet and pants and shoes and coat soaking, dripping. But I didn't even feel the cold, not yet. I raced to her. She was shivering and had this innocent, stunned stare on her face, as if to say, "What happened?"

Paul put her in his jacket, and we walked the mile back to the farmhouse where we toweled her above a heat register. I was shaking to think I'd almost lost her. I kept seeing her furry head not making it to the surface as the current was beginning to take her beneath the one opening. But I saved her. Paul kept telling me. I saved her.

As we drove home, Saba slept and I rode barefoot, my feet close to the heater, amazed that this innocent little creature had led me into a stream I have always wanted to enter. What a strange baptism for us both, and such a bonding. There was no giving her back now.

In the weeks that followed, I learned a great deal about dogs and about the nature of my fear. Much of it came from the unpredictable movement of dogs. But living with Saba, I came to understand her doggishness, began to understand how her mouth was her chief way of knowing the world. Most of all, I came to appreciate how thoroughly present she was, how there was nothing for her but the moment she was in. I loved to go on long walks in the country with her. I must admit that she opened me to the outdoors and a freedom of movement I had never known.

When people ask, "How did you overcome your fear?" I simply say, "By loving what I feared." It seems an impossible concept, but I don't know what else to say. I certainly didn't plan it, just eventually stayed open to it. But clearly, it is not the loving of what is unpleasant that restores wholeness and balance. Rather, it is the risk of loving itself that disempowers the depth of our fear, if we can only stay in the story long enough for love to show up. In truth, by undressing the things we fear, by simply loving them—no easy task—we can address the real issue: the fear of being alive in a wonder that is beyond our control. Yet opening ourselves to such wonder is impossible as long as we stay contained in the story of our fear.

It's been fourteen years, and Saba is now gone. I loved her dearly. Her thoroughness of nature led me further and further into direct living. People I've known from the beginning are amazed to hear me say so. No one can understand it. I hardly do myself. There are those who remark on my courage, but it hardly seems heroic to walk down a path so long that you are changed for the walking.

I miss that dog. She was an unexpected teacher for whom I kept stepping over the edge of my fear. For love of this simple dog, I kept having to redefine my story of life. It makes me ask: through what form of love will you step over your self-defined edge of the earth? Just how can we let the story before us unfold? How can we unfold into it? How can we plainly listen to life? How can we turn what we hear into questions that will lead us to a more truthful way of living? And how can following those questions lead us into an ever-more-clear relationship with our fear, with others, and with God?

Living within Patterns

It is a curious thing.
The river runs free
though it is contained
by the banks that it carves,
the way our love runs free,
contained by the things
that we love.

Much of life is the forming and breaking of patterns. In fact, the holy trinity of Hinduism can be seen as the elemental forces that create, sustain, and break the patterns that are necessary for life to take place. Brahma is the creator, divining patterns through which life can be carried on earth, while Vishnu is the sustainer of life and the patterns that carry it. And Shiva is the destroyer of patterns that have run their course. Shiva is the necessary instrument of transformation, breaking old life forms down so that Brahma can create new ones. In some quarters, it is believed that these powerful deities are really three distinct faces of one unnameable god.

What's crucial is to realize that these three aspects of life force are alive and working in each of us, like spiritual DNA. And we are all constantly in a process of creating, sustaining, or destroying the patterns that carry our life. Often, we suffer terribly because we resist these elemental needs. Given our stubbornness and willfulness, we often find ourselves sorely stalled in the face of change. But how we relate to these divine energies frequently determines whether or not we can find our courage at all.

It bears a lifelong learning. So I invite you to discern the patterns that are shaping your life, which of these need to be sustained or destroyed, and what new patterns need to be created. As we delve into what it means to live within patterns, I invite you to attend the story of your own life waiting to unfold. But to be clear, a constant tension lives here, as we are relentlessly creating patterns to make sense of our lives and then needing to break free of those that no longer fit who we are becoming. The goal, then, is not to eliminate that tension. That is impossible, for we are always forming, sustaining, and breaking down—always being born, living, and dying in some way. Rather, like so many of the things that matter in life, we are asked, even required, to learn how to hold that which is life sustaining though it never stands still, the way a blind man might hold water.

We need to examine the nature of patterns and how healthy ones (meaningful practices) can calcify into unhealthy ones (habitual routines). We need to consider the art of softening habitual routines back into meaningful practices. We need to discern when the rigid ones just need to be broken so our heart can once again breathe. For if we can learn the mysterious art of navigating our patterns, those rivers will guide us to our core.

A good image for all this is an *acequia*, which, in South America, is the name for a sluiceway that flows down a mountainside, providing water for a village. Just as many European cities have been built along rivers throughout the ages, many South American villages have settled around the mouth of an acequia that begins high and out of sight in the crags of a mountain. There, the source water from the gods seemingly collects all winter near the top, and, in spring, with the thaw, it streams relentlessly into the village.

When my dear friend Wayne was staying in Peru, he found himself in the middle of an annual ritual in which an entire village of eight hundred people climbed the mountain in early spring to walk and clear the acequia of rocks and tree limbs and snake nests that during the winter had blocked the path of water that the village depended on. This ancient ritual provides a wonderful model of a meaningful practice, as well as a strong metaphor of how to care for our connection to the Source.

In this story, we can see that the acequia, whose pattern down the mountain has been worn through the years, is the one direct path that keeps the village connected to the source element of water. The acequia is very much like our path of connection to Spirit and Oneness and to the source element that we call life force, which always seems to gather and replenish itself high and out of view. And if we live near the mouth of it, we are never wanting in times of need. But we must care for the acequia of Spirit from which our souls need to drink.

So keeping the acequia clear and flowing is a meaningful practice. Interestingly, the other side of life, which is inevitable and not evil, gives rise to the erosion and debris that clutters the acequia during winter—the stones and limbs that block the flow, as well as the nesting of smaller creatures. These serve as symbols of dead things that get in the way and smaller living things that take up residence smack in the middle of the flow. Wayne was amazed, when walking the acequia with the villagers, that they simply moved the nests of smaller animals. They didn't kill these creatures unless they became dangerous.

There is a powerful teaching in this. For during our recurring winters, many of the burdens we carry fall over or break off, and they clutter our connection to the Source. The inner debris that blocks the path is endless. It could consist of almost anything that weighs us down: a debilitating memory of grief or a broken stone of low esteem. And so we must regularly walk our acequia of Spirit and clear out the path.

Even more telling are the snake nests that take up residence in the acequia. These represent the poisonous tapeworms of the soul, the out-of-balance compulsions and addictions that keep us from being whole, like our insatiable hunger for power or celebrity. We simply can't let them live there. And when dangerous— when they refuse to go, when they strike at us—they must be starved, no longer fed with water from the Source. Sometimes they have to be killed.

The life of the acequia and our responsibility to keep its path of flow clear represent a cycle of erosion and cleansing that is intrinsic to everything living. Therefore, it bears learning how to do well. The heart of this book explores the many acequias that flow from the Source, the many natural obstacles that tend to block the Source, and the many rituals and practices by which people throughout the ages have cleared the path of flow.

One more thing worth noting is the model of true community that the people of this small village in Peru have given us. Whether the water coming down that mountain is actual water or the stream of a nation's reverence for life, the caring of the acequia and the sharing of the abundant flow, when it comes, is something that we, in our modern sophistications, have forgotten how to do. What an education waits for us there! And how do we resurrect such a practice today—in our families, our cities, our country, in our global village?

It seems the place to start is always within the confusion of our own days, where we find ourselves subject to both the press and comfort of the patterns that confine us. Often we can feel the Spirit underneath our habits. And deep down, we know that though the ways we have chosen have lost their freshness, our blood is fine. It's the way we clog it up that sneaks up on us. Once we're awake, the struggle is often whether we live in the world of things while glimpsing the light of Spirit or in the light of Spirit while moving through the world of things It is a practice just to be aware of which is driving us.

Inevitably, maintaining our authenticity means constantly living within patterns and breaking patterns. It is not about eliminating our humanness. Not about eliminating our want to be loved, but curbing the stubborn ways we hurt and disrespect ourselves to get that love. This involves recognizing the unhealthy patterns we fall into and correcting our course. It is not helpful to label what doesn't work as bad and then strive to rid ourselves of our very human flaws.

The aim is not to make ourselves pure and one-sided in our aliveness, but to inhabit all of who we are, living into the dilations and constrictions of our strengths and weaknesses. It is about learning how to *live through* being human, until the rhythm of being human can be celebrated as the magically imperfect vessel of Spirit that it is. Though they can be dangerous and life draining, patterns, if kept meaningful, are incubators of Spirit.

Keeping the Flow Clear

All this to say that the art of creating, sustaining, and breaking patterns in order to stay close to life is not as clean and easy as it sounds. But it is crucial to whether we will actually live the life we are given or fall into misses and echoes that we chronicle with regret. All this to say that if we can learn the mysterious art of navigating patterns, following those rivers will guide us to our core. All this to say that the cycle of life can turn healthy patterns (meaningful practices) into unhealthy ones (habitual routines). And, if that isn't hard enough, we, by being human, take turns: penetrating the illusions that confine us, only in time to narrow the gifts of our humanity until we stumble back into illusion. And so it takes courage to keep the acequia of spirit unblocked. It takes courage to keep the path of flow clear. But like a blind man holding water, we can rejoice. There is nothing like the wetness of life on our unexpecting lips.

How We Stumble

You arrive after years like a broken bird.
You are finally a breath away from everything.

What is it in our nature that, on the one hand, gives us the resources to penetrate illusion and, on the other hand, narrows the gifts of our humanity until we stumble back into illusion? It is a riddle of human nature that we are not going to solve here. Still, there is much to be gained for joining in the age-old conversation.

The great Roman orator Cicero (106–43 B.C.) offered these "Six Mistakes of Man"—six habits of thinking that keep us a prisoner of ever-shrinking patterns:

The illusion that personal gain is made up of crushing others;
The tendency to worry about things that cannot be changed or
    corrected;
Insisting that a thing is impossible because we cannot accomplish it;
Refusing to set aside trivial preferences;
Neglecting development and refinement of the mind, and not
    acquiring the habit of reading and study;
And attempting to compel others to believe and live as we do.

All these attributes replace a larger view with a smaller one. All make opaque what is clear. All reduce instead of enlarge. All heighten our isolation over our common humanity. The fact is that we can trace each of Cicero's "mistakes" to choices that are made, consciously or not, along the way. All represent habits of thinking by which we forget that we are just a small part of something larger. As we describe these shifts, it's helpful to take a personal inventory to see if and where these choices have interfered with your compassion and vitality and, ultimately, your courage.

In doing this myself, it was hard to personalize these without judging myself. For there are some of Cicero's mistakes that I trip into all the time and others (like crushing others and compelling others to live as I do) that I don't want to believe I am capable of. But it causes me to wonder. Let's move through them.

— :: —

1. *The illusion of personal gain.* To begin with, the seesaw thinking that elevates personal gain as a result of crushing others betrays the infinite sense of things. It presumes that life and its resources are finite, that there isn't enough to go around, and therefore we can only secure our piece of the pie at the expense of others. This brutal definition of success (or survival when we are cornered) comes harshly out of a fear of scarcity and death. And while there are certainly things that are finite and scarce in this world, the deeper intangibles that hold them—like compassion and worth and acceptance—are infinite and abundant, even when we are cornered.

   This brings to mind both the Kapos in concentration camps, those Jews who served as barracks foremen, crushing others to live another day, and Victor Frankl's testament to the noble spirits he witnessed during his time in the camps:

We who lived in concentration camps can remember the men who walked through the huts comforting others, giving away their last piece of bread. They may have been few in number, but they offer sufficient proof that everything can be taken from a man but one thing: the last of the human freedoms — to choose one's attitude in any given set of circumstances, to choose one's own way.

2. *The tendency to worry.* When we tend to worry about things beyond our control, which is common, we are struggling with a lack of faith in the stream of life. We have somehow lost the ability to believe in rhythms outside of our will. This can lead us to a negative self-centeredness that adheres to a false sense of responsibility for everything that happens. When caught in this thinking, it's hard to regain perspective. We can sometimes spiral from "I am responsible for keeping them happy" to "If only I had called when I thought of it, she wouldn't be sick now." Still, even knowing this, it's hard to drop our worry when overwhelmed. This is why so many traditions encourage meditation and prayer, for the safety of the moment is a hammock that can hold us, however we climb into it.

3. *Insisting that things are impossible* because we cannot accomplish them is like saying that the proverbial tree that has fallen in the forest doesn't exist because we didn't hear it fall. Or that the bridge built between warring peoples doesn't exist because we haven't crossed it. Somehow we can shrink the vastness of the world to fit the limits of our view and force everything into that tiny little box. From here, it is easier to say something is impossible than to admit our own limitations. This sort of world-in-a-thimble thinking prohibits our ability to learn anything new. It prevents us from growing or

being refreshed. Whereas humility allows us to say, "Perhaps someone stronger can lift what I can't lift . . . Perhaps we can lift it together."

4. *Trivial preferences.* It is clear that one constricting view leads to another, and when we refuse to put down our trivial preferences, we make smallness and self-centeredness a way of life. This causes us to praise sameness. And not giving an inch keeps us from knowing others or the web of life. This reminds me of a time when I was stranded, years ago, in Rochester, New York, and a friend refused to pick me up in the middle of the night because he'd already put his car in his garage. His refusal was more than silly. It damaged our friendship.

5. *Neglecting the refinement of the mind,* and I would add the heart, is a way to choose the unexamined life over a receptive, listening journey. It is a way to stay in hiding, to choose unconscious living over mindfulness, heartfulness, and awareness. Here, we remain devoted to a reactive life that avoids change. We all know someone that we love who, like a moth to a flame, always wants to meet and look into the light, but stands us up time and again. Sometimes we do this to ourselves, making dates to look honestly in the mirror and never showing up.

6. *Compelling others.* And finally, when attempting to compel others to believe and live as we do, we fall into the ever-present trap of conviction. To understand this, we must address the paradox of both sides of knowing. One side of knowing is the quest for meaning, the endless forging of what is essential into the gold of revealed truth. The other side of knowing, though, is often entrapping. This sort of

knowing results from the hardening of truth into an attachment to a particular view or belief. Frequently, conviction of this sort turns out to be the lid on the jar of knowing.

As the mindfulness teacher Jon Kabat-Zinn puts it, "If you're too convicted in your opinions or beliefs, perhaps you are a convict, imprisoned within the confines of your own understandings." His insight suggests that arriving at conclusions can be dangerous and isolating. For not only is the trap of conviction a precursor to imposing our beliefs on others, but this sort of attachment makes us bounce off life rather than move through it.

— :: —

Just why and how do we do make these choices and stumble into these mistakes again and again? It is a humbling mystery. One of the great Confucian philosophers of the Classical period in China, Hsun Tzu (300–230 B.C.), offers the fundamental reason that "whatever a person lacks in themselves they will seek outside." We always seem to look in the wrong place and stray into seeking truth amid the ten thousand things of the world, which seduce us and hypnotize us and which eventually break down our innate, holistic sense of life. It appears this is unavoidable. So our only recourse and devotion, which takes courage, is to restore our larger, deeper sense of life, again and again, by choosing or remembering our sense of the infinite, our faith in the rhythms outside of our will, and our willingness to accept our limitations and learn from the unknown. Our only remedy is to refresh our belief that meaning and love wait beneath our trivial preferences, to come out of hiding in a receptive, listening way, and to shed our convictions when they entrap us in ideas that keep us from the fresh currents of life.

The Three Dangers

Life is so beautiful.
It's the living that can be strange.
Just ask the root growing in the mud.
Or the snail thrown back by surf.

Of course, there are many ways to stumble into the patterns of
illusion. One way that patterns turn sour is by swallowing what
happens. We are so conflict averse in our culture that we will
circle the earth rather than walk directly into difference. But
unresolved conflict doesn't go away. It works on us. Even when
we internalize it and silence it, it grows in dark places like bacte-
ria. It just becomes infected. And the first danger appears when,
without having the courage to speak to those we are in conflict
with, without the strength to inquire into the situation and gain
as many views of what happened as possible, we start to fill in
the spaces all by ourselves. First, we guess at motives, as we replay
the incident from different angles, then decipher reactions, and
finally, we mix them all into a story full of judgments and warn-
ings that we have, essentially, made up in our pain.

We are all subject to this. I struggle with it constantly. It is
astonishing how quickly anyone can do this. Once we hold onto
some unexpressed slight, our need to understand what happened
and resolve it powerfully continues, whether we honor it or not.
But there is a second danger, worse than the first, and that comes

from letting our made-up story harden into the history out of which we live. As time goes by, it becomes harder and harder to break the grip of our made-up story, and the more we hold on to our own uncorroborated version of things, the more difficult it is to restore relationships. In essence, we get stuck in the version of the story we hold on to. In this way, patterns get the better of us.

This is how brothers go years without talking to each other, how friends who were inseparable now avoid parties where they might bump into each other, how co-workers mistake the clearing of a throat as an arrogant gesture sent like an arrow just for them. This is how unintended patterns solidify into walls that keep us from the messy yet miraculous life of relationships. And once our identities graft onto our solidified histories, we grow deeply invested in keeping even wrong-headed stories alive. For we fear that who we are, who we've struggled to become, will somehow dissolve, if we put the stories down—made-up or otherwise—and simply dare to begin again.

So one very difficult, but necessary courage involves taking the risk of loosening our grip on our stories—true or not— and letting them continue to unfold, even though that may be disorienting. For there is a subtle paradox at work around the stories that move our lives. It centers on the fact that living the story is when the story is most alive. As soon as an event has happened, as soon as the experience is behind us, we are asked to discern whether our story has meaning worth carrying (which is the whole point of storytelling) or whether it becomes a lifeless garment we just lug around forever, explaining to everyone we meet. The difference often depends on how open we are to being shaped by the stories we live or whether we insist on controlling and directing our stories to support our dream of things.

Yet often after making up our own version of experience in order to maintain a truce with all that is unresolved in our heart, and after letting the story harden into a history we keep defending, a third danger arises in which we cease to know the difference between what really happened and our fictional version of it. The French playwright André Gide puts it harshly, but to the point, "The true hypocrite is the one who ceases to perceive his deception, the one who starts to lie with sincerity."

I would hold this with less judgment. It is more a matter of falling, as we do, into unhealthy patterns where we let our pain insulate our understanding of life at all costs. And I am certain that, at any moment in which we are loved or forced into relaxing all we hold up, we can glimpse the truth of who we are. And when we've stumbled into a complete, if momentary, safety, that complete safety will allow us to restore the heart of our journey. I'm reminded of the Turkish proverb that says, "No matter how far you have gone on the wrong road, you can turn back."

My first real struggle with the three dangers came when I was eighteen and heading to college. For the last two years of high school, I was diving and drowning in the heat of my first love. I was completely smitten. She was a year older, and so she crossed the threshold into the larger world before me. Our soft cocoon began to tear. By the winter of my first year away, she had broken up with me. I was, of course, devastated and had no reference for what to do with such unexpected pain. I remember wandering through the snowy cemeteries of upstate New York late at night, trying to find a quiet moment that might stop the ache. But nothing helped. It felt impossible to talk with her about all this, and so, in dark hours late in the night, I began to retell our story to those kind enough to listen. I wasn't sure which hurt more, the absence of such sweet love or being so summarily rejected. They were, of course, braided.

For some reason, it felt difficult to admit and voice what actually happened. By spring, the first danger had taken hold, and I was reporting to those who hadn't heard my woe that Chris and I were both reassessing our relationship. By summer, I was saying that we both had agreed to go our separate ways for a while. And by the following fall, I was even saying to new friends that *I* had left her. All the while, my heart felt savaged, and, when alone, I would cry at what felt like an irreplaceable loss.

Within a year, the second danger took hold, and I cultivated a mythology of my first love that was beautiful and tragic. I had plotted a deep love marred by incompatibilities that forced me to let her go. Such a myth brought me great sympathy as a young man who could love enough that he would let what he loved go. The truth is that none of this was conscious.

I am humbled to say that for almost twenty years and through the course of two marriages, I slowly succumbed to the third danger and believed the version of the story that I had wrapped like a bandage around the innermost part of my heart. Was I a hypocrite as Gide suggests? From the outside, perhaps. But from the inside, there was less intent and more confusion in how to live through heartache and not retreat from the world.

It was late in my second marriage that I found myself drifting in a rowboat by myself on a summer lake. It was early. No one else was up. And for some reason, my soul had finally caught up with my personality. Or rather, I think my personality finally exhausted itself and collapsed around my ever-waiting center. But in that rare moment of congruence, I didn't need my made-up stories anymore. And without any willful decision or conscious effort, I was awakened to the truth that I had been beautifully loved and horribly left and hurt as a young man. And the story that I'd been stuck in for so many years cracked open like a shell, and I felt a refreshed directness of feeling in simply breathing, which I hadn't felt for a long time.

Facing Ourselves

Consciously or unconsciously, we avoid facing things as they
are in themselves and so we want God to open a door for us
which is beyond . . . (But) to find life's purpose we must go
through the door of ourselves.

❖ *Krishnamurti*

Why face ourselves? Because the self is the only opening through
which we can know the stuff of life and how it makes up the
world. Being human, experience clogs up the sacred opening
of self. Without facing ourselves, the self remains filmed over
and small and very little gets through, and even that essential
trickle stops touching us. It is only through the rinsed-out self
that we can experience compassion and truth. For sure, love and
suffering can rinse out the self. But these, too, can be siphoned
through our walls. What saves us from ourselves is the power of
our own honest gaze, which remains a cleansing agent that can
wash out whatever thickens within us and wash off whatever
grows over us. As a cleansing agent, self-reflection is indispensable to staying fully alive. We wouldn't think of going more than
a few days without washing and showering. So think of facing
ourselves as spiritual hygiene. For the clogged up self is the petty
self, the one who ventures into the world and only finds "me."
But the cleansed self is the transparent self, the one who feels the

aliveness and pain in everything. This is the self that serves as an inlet to the world, always feeling what moves through.

This is all hard enough, and yet we often narrow our inlet and cover our openings. We do this every time we strap on a mask or persona. We do this every time we fashion a facsimile of ourselves and wear it as a splash guard against the unexpected. With this in mind, it seems the antidote to saving face is putting face down. Ultimately, this involves removing our masks, no matter how uncanny the likeness or how good the fit. For masks clog us up and film us over, too. Of course, we think we need masks for protection. But one lesson I keep learning in my time on earth is that often the thing we mask, because we fear it won't survive if left out in the open, has the strength we need to move through life. The irony is that the strength we hide is like a match—it needs to strike off something in the open to ignite.

It took many attempts, but when I put aside the stories others had written for me, I finally removed my mask, and there was my skin wanting for light. When suffering removed my skin, there was the muscle and bone that had carried me through time. When time removed the muscle and bone, there was the river of life that had kept me alive. When the river of life stilled itself, I could see through to the bottom of everything, waiting to be stirred. This took many lifetimes. To my surprise, the only way to cut through in this lifetime is to love and be loved. For love is the only thing that cuts the work of time in half. And facing ourselves is the surest way to ready ourselves for love.

As with many things that matter, though, there is work to be engaged before the work. In order to face ourselves, we must face life. In order to face life, we must face death. In his compelling and mysterious apprenticeship with the sorcerer Don Juan, Carlos Castenada is told that death is an advisor: that it sits over our left shoulder, insuring the uniqueness of every thing we behold. Now we can become transfixed with the fact that every living thing will die, or we can become enlivened by the fact that every thing we face is utterly unrepeatable. This is no small threshold to cross each day. But when we can enter the realm of utter uniqueness, that fact alone demands that we bring our best and truest self to each thing we face. This is the mysterious doorway to meaning, and the price of admission is nothing less than our fullest nature, opened by the practice of facing ourselves. In beautiful symmetry, what is found on the inside of all that is unrepeatable is the lifeblood of the true self.

Despite the countless distractions and obstacles we face each day, life is a journey of approaching a horizon that we never arrive at. The journey is sometimes made alone, sometimes with others. But the approach, over a lifetime, if faced openly and honestly, hones us into an instrument of living that turns suffering into a music that is bewitching and healing, a music we call love. And, if blessed to endure the distractions and move through the obstacles, we discover a curious law of inner alchemy: the closer we get to light, the more fully we are lighted. The closer we get to truth and beauty, the more truthful and beautiful we become. In the same way, the closer we get to that sacred meadow called death, the more and more alive we grow. And the more we live in the sanctity that life and death reveal in each other, the more loving we grow.

If any of this makes sense to you, you might be asking, *how? How do we face ourselves?* It is an elusive art at best, and I do not pretend to have expertise—just a lifetime of failed attempts, which, oddly, have their own beauty when left in the light. But one thing is clear: the self, faced cleanly, opens many things. It is the one place we have left to try when all other paths fail. As the Argentinean writer Jorge Luis Borges says, "Any life, no matter how long and complex it may be, is made up of a single moment—the moment in which a person finds out, once and for all, who they are."

The Life of the Lion

How I w-w-wish I had some c-c-courage . . .
‹ the Lion in *The Wizard of Oz*

En route to facing ourselves, we encounter a ravine we must cross, much like the ravine in which Jacob wrestles with the unnamed angel in order to go on. It is here that we establish our relationship to strength and power, qualities that can help us enjoin the living or destroy ourselves and everything we touch. Throughout history, this wrestling with strength and power has been characterized in the mythology of the lion.

Nearly all cultures have stories of the lion which represent the best and worst of what it means to be human. From the Egyptian sphinx that guards the sun to the fire-breathing Chimera of Greece that burns everything it breathes on, from the Chinese lion that chases evil spirits to the horrendous and impenetrable Nemean lion that Hercules slew, from the sea lions of northern Canada who nurse those lost at sea to the role of Buddha as the tamer of lions in men (*Purusa-damya-sarathi*), the lion has inspired us to our courage and vigilance and warned us against our brutality and greed.

Most stories throughout the ages lift up the lion, or the lion-like, as either the one who embodies and liberates or the one who consumes and turns brutal. Often, there is a strength and power that faces the brutal and a misuse of that strength and power that can turn brutal. In essence, there is always the lion energy fulfilled (the lionhearted) and the shadow of that energy run amok (the king of the jungle). This is not just an idea, but an important dynamic of reality that we each need to understand as we enter our days. For both energies live in each of us, and we can respond with either in an instant to whatever situation is before us.

Indeed, the life of the lion has been a story throughout time of our relationship to strength and power, which enlarges when we are connected and sharpens when we are cut off. When we can find our core and stand by it, a connective, embodied power arises that unifies the living. Such embodiments can be heroic in the deepest sense. Yet when we grow lost or numb and are cut off from that core, the power grips and consumes us. It uses *us* up in the endless extension and replication of itself at all cost. Such is the sanctity of being centered and the eyeless authority of having no center. The connective power embodies and serves the Whole, while the consuming power grips and serves the part. And we are often left in the middle, being pulled by both.

In truth, the journeys of facing the lion and being the lion are inescapable, part of an archetypal passage that everyone must go through, whether we arrive in life as a leader of armies or the mother of twelve. In this regard, facing the lion and being the lion are initiations by which we discover and tend our place in the Universe. When facing the lion of our potential, we are called to enter a journey of individuation and discovery through which we can find our core. Not surprisingly, at the center, our core and the Source reveal their Oneness. The strength realized from touching on that Oneness is the strength of the lion manifest in the world.

At the same time, we are called to face the unleashed power of the lion run amok. In this regard, facing the lion often involves standing up to things and people who, in not standing by their core, have become agents that dishearten all they touch. In these moments, they become voracious, life-draining shadows of the lion. And we are charged to stand by our core in order not be trodden by this energy. It is a function of universal balance that calls us to face the lion turned brutal.

More deeply, facing the lion is the call to summon our best qualities in order to face some one, some thing, some force that is challenging. But this one or thing or force is not always bad or dangerous, as life often demands that we face things in order to transform—a process we often resist. If persistent, facing our challenges can transform us into our truest self. So *to face* does not mean *to resist or defeat*, but *to encounter honestly*. And *to be* does not mean *to retreat from the world*, but *to merge with it from a centered place of strength*.

Now an immediate paradox presents itself as soon as we attempt to both face the lion and be the lion. The paradox is: When *we* are the lion, do others fear facing *us*? Just when are we stubborn and imposing? And when are we humble instruments for another's inevitable transformation? At our best, we serve as inadvertent triggers for each other's eventual illumination. At our worst, we blindly oppress others and keep them from being who they are called to be. I don't believe any of us consciously do this, though if some do, I would call their deliberate act of suppression evil. So it is not enough to simply be a lion. We have to work hard not to mistreat others with our strength once we find it.

Two contemporary myths that speak to all of this are the popular epics, *Star Wars* and *Lord of the Rings*. Both unfold ancient themes about strength, power, and courage. In *Star Wars*, the generational twining of the dark and light side of the force, as competing ways of being, harks all the way back to Cain and Abel. Instead of brothers resisting and loving each other, we have a father and son doing so. And while the force is never fully defined, it echoes the universal ground of being at the center of every spiritual tradition. It is tantamount to the Tao, the mysterious stream of life that releases its infinite power when we can align with it. The dark side implies the destructive chaos that seems to always be unleashed when we—through fear, greed, and arrogance—try to capture the infinite in a bottle for our own use. It is the intoxicated ego that often does harm by thinking it can direct and manipulate something too powerful to ever be controlled, like trying to thread a needle with lightning.

In *The Lord of the Rings*, however, J. R. R. Tolkien boldly creates a new story in which he says that the power itself can never be trusted, regardless of its source or our relationship to it. And so the courage for young Frodo is to destroy the ring that releases the power, so that no one can wear it and be tempted into brutality. As we look at the dark side of human history, Tolkien may prove the wisest among us.

Yet these ageless physics of being in the world may not speak to you. Still, you may ask: Why face the lion? Why be the lion? In answer, I offer the passionate insight of Martin Luther King, Jr., who revealed an inextricable link between power and love:

Power properly understood is nothing but the ability to achieve purpose. And one of the great problems of history is that the concepts of love and power have usually been contrasted as opposites—polar opposites—so that love is identified with a resignation of power, and power with a denial of love.

We've got to get this thing right. What is needed is a realization that power without love is reckless and abusive, and love without power is sentimental and anemic. Power at its best is love implementing the demands of justice, and justice at its best is power correcting everything that stands against love. It is precisely this collision of immoral power with powerless morality which constitutes the major crisis of our time.

So here we are and, regardless of our position in life, we each will come into contact with power. Like it or not, we can no more avoid it than the air we need to breathe. As with air, we must inhale and exhale strength and power to live. The question has always been: how do we define these elements? Is strength the art of authority, of achieving dominion over situations and others, as rulers throughout history have maintained? Or is strength the art of embrace, of surrendering to the power of love and truth rising up within us, as spiritual elders throughout history have offered? Or is the secret of power an elusive braiding of capacities we don't understand? Regardless of our preference or insight or ignorance, we *have* to be in relationship to these elements. That this is so seems a koan imprinted by God into the journey of life. And so what is it we are to learn from this journey? It is a dangerous set of lessons, to be sure.

We all carry the seed of each element: the power of authority and the power of embrace. When broken or humbled, we move from one to the other. It was a German monk named Schwarz who, in 1369, devised the idea of propelling a projectile with gunpowder. And so the first handgun shot its first bullet. But what caused a contemplative to create a gun? Why did he trade inner power for outer power? And five hundred years later, Alfred Nobel signed his last will and testament in Paris. With it, he tried to compensate for unleashing dynamite on the world by creating the Nobel Prizes, including the Peace Prize, first awarded in 1901 and funded with money earned from selling dynamite. What made him want to counter the outer power he let loose on the world?

In one way, the journey can be reduced to this challenge: to either be *of God*—that is, to be in kinship to everything larger than us, in alignment with the Whole—or to be *Godlike*, as in being the creator and ruler over all that we see. The difference has defined the twin rivers of history: those who have yearned to become wholehearted and complete, in the image of God, committed to all ways of knowing, though we can never be all knowing, and those who have yearned to assume God's position, to be a god, and conquer or possess the world. Though the challenge seldom presents itself this starkly. More often, we are tempted to trudge after geese in the snow until we have a clear shot, only to find that the trigger has frozen, and, reluctantly, we put down our gun and just listen to them flutter off, to where we secretly would like to go.

Facing Each Other

Conveyed from mouth to ear, there is no tradition. There are
no textbooks. There is only direct meeting, direct experience.
There is no practice without a teacher. There is no teacher without a community. There are souls destined to meet—and free
will and commitment, and loving-kindness and fellowship. And
out of these branches the path.

❖ *Perle Besserman*

The Buddhist teacher Jack Kornfield speaks of an ancient custom among nomadic peoples, among Bedouins and gypsies, a
ritual that is an inoculation against staying a stranger. Since these
peoples moved about often and quickly, they needed a quick,
direct, and honest way to be in relationship with those they met
along the way. So the custom of getting to know another always
began with three simple questions: *Who are you? Where are you
from? Where are you in your journey?*

As for me, I have been blessed to have good friends. One reason,
I think, is that in addition to being there for each other, we inquire into each other. Without realizing it, we receive each other
as inner gypsies, always eager to ask the three simple questions.
We tend to climb each other the way we would a rocky coast to
get that undeniable view of the sea. And then we wait, to listen
to that sea, to watch how God tosses it about. We scale down to
the sands to see what the storms have cast ashore. Though we

know each other well, and though there are times we can finish each other's sentences or watch a situation unfold and whisper to one another, "There he goes again," we mostly wake like the Bedouins and look into each other's eyes and ask, *Who are you? Are you alive? Just what is that like?*

To face each other in this way and to ask such questions is quietly heroic. It takes remembering that life is unrepeatable and that living isn't guaranteed. It requires listening to what comes back, even when it doesn't make sense. It is often the courage to ask that keeps us going and the courage to sip from each other that keeps us well. For when a friend sits with you and asks, "Where have you been and what are you seeing from your small quarter of eternity?" that kind of love turns the secret inside out.

In truth, we are each a country unto ourselves, made of the same earth, with the same water streaming through; each with a language all our own, learned in the interior, each worth knowing. And as the roots of all river trees know only one water, the roots of all feelings know only one heart. So open the country of your heart when you are cold and I'll open mine, till we dream ourselves warm, till we sip the one water.

This all invokes the courage to stay in conversation with each other, to stay in relationship with each other through the moments when we're terribly human and stumbling toward our better selves through the messiness of our lesser selves. To be clear, I am not advocating that we stay in abusive situations, but that, while taking care of ourselves, we keep assessing and discerning what it means to stay real in each other's company. For just as we return to the breath in the practice of meditation, we return to the breath of authenticity in the practice of relationship.

In this regard, facing each other has much to do with James Hillman's notion of absorbing each other's images:

If the character of a person is a complexity of images, then to know you I must imagine you, absorb your images. To stay connected with you, I must stay imaginatively interested, not in the process of our relationship or in my feelings for you, but in my imaginings of you. The connection through imagination yields an extraordinary closeness.

Every day, we are offered chance after chance to practice staying in relationship to the many forms of life that feed us, mirror us, and connect us. More than mentally receiving each other, this involves daring to imagine each other freshly through the heart.

In a daily way, the aim of true dialogue is not to arrive at a truce or even a compromise, though these are instrumental, but to strive for a fundamental understanding of each other that reconfigures the geography of everyone involved, regardless of the issue, without anyone losing or sacrificing their core. Over time, conversations of this order carve a riverbed between human beings for Source to flow to Source. To create this interpersonal riverbed—to make it clear, flowing, and lasting—takes time and a commitment to sustain the effort to listen and to not act prematurely. Being in that river together is the point. As Hannah Arendt says, "It is when we are in dialogue that we are most human."

It is interesting that the word *interview*, from the French, means *the view between, to see each other*. The medical sociologist Richard Frankel notes that before widespread literacy, the *interview* was the prevalent method and most meaningful way of communicating with each other—in person, face to face. And while there is no question that the written word has gifted us with an immense acceleration of knowledge, we have been compensating for the loss of direct, face-to-face exchange ever since. We are so busy and list driven that we have lost the art of "the view between."

I fall prey to this as much as anyone. The other day, up early, getting ready for work, reordering my to-do list in my head, I chanced to look at my wife Susan and our dog asleep in the dark. It made me smile to think how sometimes our dog gets that look in her eye and starts running full speed in circles and crazy eights, leaping over flowers and through the aging trees. I looked back to Susan. She was under the covers, her cheek showing, our dog curled in the crook of her legs, as close as she could get. I beheld them, in the dimness, wondering how anything could be so at rest. And in their sleep, our dog twitched, dreaming of running, as Susan smiled, dreaming of her garden growing.

There I was, half dressed in the half light, absorbing their images. It made me realize what super powers we've been given—to ripple in motion and know the inside of air, to stand in the dark and watch what we love, to sleep with animals and simply dream, and to see for the first time, more than once. Sometimes what seems ordinary exposes its numinous bone, the way a man worn to love can grow in the dark, just by aching for words.

Sympathetic Fibers

We cannot live for ourselves alone. Our lives are connected
by a thousand invisible threads, and along these sympathetic
fibers, our actions run as causes and return to us as results.
❖ *Herman Melville*

When we can bring our best and truest self to each thing we
face, we have our best chance at being lionhearted. One reward for our fidelity to compassion is that the sympathetic fibers
that Melville refers to become visible—only to those who open
their hearts. So facing ourselves can exercise our innate strength
of heart, which, in turn, can make the fabric of the Universe visible. This is why we are often called to serve or bear witness to
the suffering of strangers: to discover the strength and wisdom
in connection.

Though we are tugged into acts of compassion, the pull often remains invisible. One courage that is always before us is
whether to dismiss the pull of these invisible threads as illogical
nightmares or to follow them as beautiful manifestations of how
we all need each other. I have a friend, Kate Dahlstedt, who was
living a fine life as a therapist in upstate New York when one of
the invisible threads tugged at her. Now she is in South Africa,
helping those dying and those left behind in the massive AIDS
epidemic there. She writes of her first days:

We start out this morning and right off we see a monkey along the road, just like squirrels at home. Much of our travel is on dirt roads and grassy paths. At our first stop the patient has died. The little room has candles lit and six women all sitting on the floor mourning, the wife completely wrapped in a blanket, as the custom is for her not to speak to anyone.

The next day a caregiver tells me a story about a mother who had no food to feed her hungry children, so she put a pot of water on the fire and told them that she was cooking some meat that would take a long time. She kept telling them this when they cried and finally they fell asleep. The next morning they asked her again and she told them they had fallen asleep and missed it . . . I am already changed.

In his book *At Hell's Gate*, Claude Anshin Thomas recounts the heartbreaking journey that led him into the truth of our connectedness. As a nineteen year old, he went to Vietnam. The killing turned him into a drug addict. Upon his return, he eventually became homeless, and, through a series of painful and courageous awakenings, he took refuge as a Zen monk. It is a remarkable story, and from the other end of that harrowing climb, he offers this lesson:

If I recognize the interconnectedness of all beings, then I can come to a place of understanding, a place beyond the intellect, a place where I am not separate from anything. And here I . . . discover that my actions have an impact on the whole world.

We inevitably have the chance, like Kate and Claude, to realize the sympathetic fibers that connect us. This doesn't require travel, though it often requires a journey. Through love and suffering, we can know that there are, in fact, two umbilical cords at birth: the one that is cut so that we can live and, paradoxically, the unseeable one that is never cut, through which the very force of life keeps reviving us, if we let it. Paradoxically, the cord that is cut lets us be personal in the world, while the one that is never cut lets us transcend what is personal. There is no question we need both paths to live fully and to make a difference.

These notions are not new, but rooted in various traditions. The Navajo say that seeking wholeness is personal, an individual journey, while seeking harmony is transpersonal, a communal journey. This ethic bears a kinship to the two Buddhist traditions: Hinayana Buddhism, which seeks personal enlightenment (*Hinayana* means *little raft*), and Mahayana Buddhism, which seeks a mutual enlightenment with others (*Mahayana* means *big raft*). As well, the Navajo word *Ahyo-oh'-oh-ni* means *to bring one into harmony with everything*. This is a key purpose of Native American education, based on the indigenous notion of *All My Relations*, which views all of reality and life as related and interconnected.

A similar approach to life can be found in the African view of *Ubuntu*, which is often translated as *I am because you are, you are because I am*. It implies finding our humanity in each other. Archbishop Desmond Tutu says that "Ubuntu is the essence of being human: that my humanity is caught up in your humanity." And Dirk J. Louw, from the University of the North in South Africa, tells us that "Ubuntu is a Zulu word that serves as the spiritual foundation of African societies. It is a unifying vision that comes from the Zulu maxim *umuntu ngumuntu ngabantu*, which literally means *a person is a person through other persons*."

Through many paths, we are led to a devotion and discernment of relationship that takes us through self and beyond self into the interdependent mystery where, as the Hindus say, "Thou Art That," where we find ourselves in each and every living thing.

Indra's Net

The image of Indra's net is an ancient way of understanding what Melville speaks of as "invisible threads" and what Henry David Thoreau calls "the infinite extent of our relations." It gives us a meaningful way to understand the living structure of reality.

Indra is the Hindu god who symbolizes the natural forces that protect and nurture life, and it is said that above the palace of Indra you can see an infinite net. No one has seen it all, but it is said to cover the earth, suspended like an atmosphere. At each knot in the net there is a clear and radiant jewel that reflects all the other jewels. And each jewel contains and mirrors the entire net and all the jewels that hold the net together.

Through the lenses of physics, biology, psychology, and spirit, Indra's net is a metaphor for how each living part contains the whole and how the smallest unit of energy—be it an atom, cell, psyche, or soul—is crucial to binding the threads of life. These irreducible units of life are the clear, brilliant jewels holding the infinite net together. This is why when we love, we touch the love of everything, and when we suffer, we touch the history of all suffering. In this way, Indra's net helps us to understand our inextricable connection to everything and everyone. For the slightest shift in one part of the net influences the movement of the entire net. In truth, we are, at our best, clear jewels holding the invisible threads of the living together. Each of us is such a jewel or knot, depending on whether our spirit is clear and radiant or filmed over by unprocessed experience.

But what if we can't see the Universe and its net of connections? It might mean that the jewel of our soul is filmed over by the unavoidable process of living. It might mean we are in need of clarifying agents that will wipe the jewel of our spirit clean and restore its ability to be clear and brilliant and utterly reflective of all other life. This returns us to the purpose of all the spiritual practices in the wisdom traditions, which, in their own way, aim to restore the transparency of spirit that lets the forces of life move through our hearts and minds, the way blood rejuvenates the body. And it is not by accident that love remains the best cleansing agent of all time.

The image of Indra's net also reveals the dynamics of the individual soul. In the same way that a body is made up of organs, and organs are made up of tissues, imagine that as the net of life is held together by clear jewels, each jewel or soul is held together by its own net of smaller jewels. Perhaps these gems are our living capacities, our aspects of soul—such as generosity, integrity, and loving-kindness, to name a few. Perhaps these are the smaller jewels within us that, when kept clear, contain and reflect our life of endless connection and so restore our place in the Universe.

The spiritual equation is stark in its truth. When clear as a jewel, we are connected to everything. When not, we are knotted and filled with tensions. Yet if one laughs in the forest, and it causes another to smile in his sleep, isn't the Universe a blessed playground? And if one is wounded in the city, and the wound causes another to wake with a nightmare, isn't the Universe a net of irresistible compassion? And if you and I, complaining about our taxes, step over the homeless without even seeing them, don't we absorb their plight just the same? The threads of Indra's net are finer than silk and stronger than centuries. We are tied to each other in ways no one person can fully understand, and we are each called to exercise the courage to stay clear and connected.

The Shekinah Is in Exile

There is an ancient Jewish notion that holds the paradox and promise of our life of endless connection, which the Jewish tradition names as the Divine Presence of God. It suggests that such Divine Presence is indwelling and dormant in each of us, and dormant between us as well. It suggests that this Indwelling Presence between human beings is a synonym for God. But the paradox is that the indwelling face of God is in exile in the world—unless we enliven it. The Jewish name for this indwelling face of God is *Shekinah*. We are told by Talmudic Rebbes that in small towns in Eastern Europe, before the Holocaust, criers would go about at dawn knocking at shutters like holy roosters, declaring, "Get up, sweet, holy Jews! The Shekinah is in exile!"

This speaks to a lineage in the wisdom traditions that affirms that when we find and enliven our own center, we also find and enliven the common center between all human beings, and that striking those sympathetic fibers among living things finds and enlivens the very heart of God.

In this respect, standing by one's core also means standing by the core of mystery. One enlivens the other. And this deep resonance allows us to know, however briefly, the Indwelling Presence by which all living things know each other. It's as if in lining up the center of our days with the center of our soul, we also align with the center of all life, and when all those centers align, the mystery lets go a sigh that is the music of the spheres.

The paradox is that each of us is capable of ignoring or chasing the Shekinah from the world. This is the basic tension of being a spirit in the world: that we can illuminate or obscure the irreducible elements of life. Herein lies the whole purpose of the little will we have: to let the Indwelling Presence thrive in the light until it is no longer indwelling. This is the courage beneath all courage.

And regardless of our willingness to accept or deny the fact of it, we are all on a journey that requires us to never cut the unseeable cord that ties us to everything, a journey that invites us to honor our endless life of connection, a journey that challenges us to stay clear and unclouded, a journey that needs us to bring the Indwelling Presence we all carry out into the world.

A very touching story from the Talmud captures the soft paradox of all these aspects of the journey. A rabbi asks his students, "How do you know the first moment of dawn has arrived?" After a great silence, one pipes up, "When you can tell the difference between a sheep and a dog." The rabbi shakes his head no. Another offers, "When you can tell the difference between a fig tree and an olive tree." Again, the rabbi shakes his head no. There are no other answers. The rabbi circles their silence and walks between them, "You know the first moment of dawn has arrived, when you look into the eyes of another human being and see yourself."

The Art of Encouragement

As a friend, it began with her pointing
to the wonders along the way. Now, she
surfaces from time to time, a wonder
herself, glistening with the deep.

There is an art to imparting strength and confidence, to inspiring and heartening what is already within us. In many ways, to
encourage is to help the heart unfold. And each time we do
so, another aspect of our true self unfolds. Very often, the art of
encouragement is needed to counter some sort of fear, which
blocks us from what we already know. Fear makes courage forget
itself. Encouragement reminds us of what we're capable of.

In the modern classic *The Wizard of Oz*, the lion is afraid of
everything and is sorely in need of courage—not to be heroic,
but simply to make it through the days. So he joins Dorothy, the
tin man, and the scarecrow—all off to see the wizard. In particular, the lion hopes the wizard can magically give him some courage. En route, he is tested in unexpected ways, and, though afraid,
he manages to cope quite bravely. Once in the Emerald City,
the wizard not only informs the lion that he can't give him any
courage, but he confesses that he is fearful himself. Still, he does
give the lion the gift of telling him that the courage he seeks has
been inside of him all along. This, of course, is a contemporary

myth that holds the fear we all experience and the truth we all need. It reflects the timeless quandary between fear and courage, between withdrawing from what we know and standing by one's core. Experientially, fear and courage are like two lovers who beckon us constantly, promising us everything. And though we're always startled to learn that there is no wizard, in the end, we're grateful to learn that fear and courage are already at home within us, tools for us to clean and use.

So I want—*and need*—to explore the relationship between fear and courage, between acting on what we know and standing by one's core. For each of us, like the lion making his way through Oz, has to live with fear and still act on what we know; sometimes to be heroic as life and love demand, but mostly just to make it through the days. On a more subtle, but just as crucial level, we all need to stand by our respective cores, in order to keep the world possible. It is an age-old truth that when we can stand by our core and act on what we know, we keep ourselves and the web of life intact. Each time courage finds its face in the middle of fear, the world grows.

Looking at Life Together

There is a poetry in looking at life together. I have a friend who wrote me about the meaning of a poem I sent her. It really doesn't matter which poem or what it said. The reason I mention this is that, as the "author," I don't have any advantage in uncovering its meaning. I just write poems—that is, receive them—trying to stay out of the way, trying not to corrupt what comes through with too many of my own preferences for meaning. The fact is that my interpretation is no more clear or relevant than anyone else's. Actually, the poems instruct and lead me. My friend's guess is as good as mine. It is really the conversations that arise from circling what is retrieved, openly and honestly, that mark the real poetry. In this, we are all poet-fishermen, netting experience as we go and dumping what we catch and drag on deck, to look at it together.

The entire process makes me think of Jackson Pollack's method of painting, how he would let the brush hover over the canvas, not directly touching it but letting the paint have the space to free-fall and find its deeper flow. He wasn't just throwing paint, but giving up his predeterminations of where the paint belonged. Instead, he entered a relationship with the space in between his brush and the painting. Honoring this space allowed deeper patterns to land on the canvas.

It is this interplay with the space between that Martin Büber spoke of as the space of true dialogue. Or, as he put it, the space of I-Thou, where unrehearsed dialogue with God arises between two living centers. Letting go of our predeterminations and honoring the space between is what allows the meaning of life to find its deeper expression between us. The poetry exists in that space between—between the poet and the Source, between the one living and their experience, and then between the two or more who try to make sense of it.

Ultimately, we know very little without each other. Ultimately, we need each other to understand. This is the terrain of encouragement. The wonderful poet Denise Levertov makes this freshly clear in her poem *The Secret*. There, she recounts how two young girls rush to her, giddy to tell her that they have discovered the secret of life in a line of one of her poems.

Ecstatic, they thank her and run off. But Levertov aches to know which line in which poem! Alone without the secret, she blesses the two girls for their discovery and for believing that there is a secret in the first place. That belief alone imparts strength and confidence to her. And the world grows.

Let it Come to You
Nature cannot be forced, but only loved into visibility.
❖ Irene Manton

Maureen O'Hara, the former president of the Saybrook Institute, tells how her mentor changed her life with a simple, gentle, clear instruction. She was studying biology at the University of Leeds with Irene Manton, the first female to ever use an electron microscope. After four days of trying to see a cell, Maureen, frustrated, cursed the bloody thing, and Dr. Manton put her hand on Maureen's shoulder and offered from a place of practiced wonder, "O Maureen, you won't see it if you hate it. You will only see it if you love it. Then it will come to you. Let it come to you."

Such a gentle, profound lesson. It is not enough to recognize the larger order—*we must love it*. We must not just look at it, but appreciate it, move toward it with awe, and then, that awe emits its own gravity which pulls everything into view. It is a gravity that confirms our place in the Universe. This is why sincerity, curiosity, and gratitude are such strong, compelling tools of the heart, which, when inhabited, bring us back into the web of life where we can feel how everything is connected.

Maureen goes on to speak of how this small moment has affected how she views risk. In a world where risk is always considered in terms of transgressions, we often manage what we try, so as not to violate others, be judged, or get in trouble. But *loving our way into the web of life,* being fully alive requires us to consider what will be missed if we *don't* try, if we don't take the risk. So we have an equal if not greater need to enhance risk, so as not to slip into a lifeless watching of life passing us by. These notions, about love and risk as forces that join us in the web of life, have huge implications for how we understand education.

This is why sincerity, curiosity, and gratitude set the larger order of things in motion. As W. H. Murray says, "The moment one definitely commits oneself, then Providence moves too. All sorts of things occur to help one that would never otherwise have occurred. A whole stream of events issues from the decision which no one could have dreamed would have come their way." And the world grows.

Seeking a Guide: Being a Guide

The word *imam* is a Muslim salutation honoring someone as a spiritual guide. And what is a guide but someone who encourages us into deeper relationship with our self and with the spirit of life that gives rise to the self? In deep ways, friendship is the vocation of seeking truth together. It is the call to find meaning in life in the trusted company of others.

The Jungian analyst Helen Luke strongly asserts that we take turns seeking a guide and being a guide. But either way, she declares, "It is most surely true that no one can safely enter the dark gate of the shadow world without knowing that some deeply loved and trusted *person* has absolute faith in the rightness of their journey and in their courage and ability to come through."

Like the poet who stumbled onto the secret of life and the young girls who found it in one of her poems, we sorely need each other's belief. And how we take turns. In the stormy seas that overtake us, we rely on each other to keep our heads above water. In the Hawaiian tradition, families and friends often swim long distances together, and when one becomes injured or exhausted, the others will keep the tired one afloat, massaging them in the water before the group swims on. This act of keeping the tired one afloat while massaging their exhausted limbs is called *lomi-lomi*. They stop, tread water, and encourage their loved one to keep swimming.

This is an apt metaphor for the art of encouragement: keeping each other afloat when we're tired, keeping each other swimming, and guiding each other back into the current. The psychologist Ira Progoff puts it this way, "Love depends upon the capacity to reach beneath the surface of persons, to feel and touch the seed of life that is hidden there. And love becomes a power when it is capable of evoking that seed and drawing it forth from its hiding place." O how we take turns. And the world grows.

Standing by One's Core

Solitude does not mean living apart from others; it means never living apart from one's self.

❖ *Parker Palmer*

As I mentioned early on, the original use of the word *courage* means *to stand by one's core*. It was coming upon this image of courage that stirred me to write this book in the first place. I mean "write" in the sense of explore and unfold. As will happen, from time to time, one image or insight will rearrange how we see and understand the life we find ourselves in. Then, if we take up that mysterious curriculum, it will lead us to new understandings. And so, after many questions and conversations, you and I meet in these pages.

To stand by one's core is the central koan, the obvious riddle to be experienced, not solved. I only know that, since coming upon it, it feels essential and alive, and that this entire endeavor is my attempt to stay close to that energy, whether I ultimately understand it or not. I only know that when I think of those I've admired most, they are human beings who have been or are thoroughly themselves. By that, I do not mean individuals strong in their opinions or persuasions. Nor do I mean those who overpower others with their manner. Glimpsing someone thoroughly being their true self is akin to catching a peony the moment it opens in the sun. It is like watching for an eagle and being stopped by a hawk, full spread, gliding over all your doubts. Being in the presence of someone courageous enough to hold nothing back is like witnessing the perfect curl of surf give itself over to a thirsty shore. It is always stunning and subtle, essential and elusive. It refreshes my own courage and sense of being here.

So what are the instruments of courage? What are the instruments of standing by one's core? Instruments in the sense of tools that make courage possible and in the sense of instruments that give voice to courage. Much of this book is trying to uncover these instruments and how to use them. They are everywhere. In the shovel that digs into the earth and the honest cry that digs open the soul. Within and without, we need all the instruments we can find.

It's interesting that in founding Naropa University in Boulder, Colorado, the Tibetan Buddhist teacher Chögyam Trüngpa saw the university as a pilot light for all traditions, viewing heart and practice as the vital energies that keep the pilot light lit. Whether you are inclined to the Buddhist tradition or not, this is an apt metaphor for standing by one's core. In regard to our souls, it is essential for each of us to learn: What is that pilot light for us? What form of heart and practice keeps it lit? And what can that pilot light illuminate, warm, and ignite in the world?

In the Middle East, the Aramaic word for heart, *lebak*, comes from a root that means *passion, courage,* and *vitality*. It literally refers to *the heart or center of one's life.* And the Sufi word for inner consciousness is *sirr. Lebak* and *sirr*—the consciousness of one's core. If we are to stay vitally alive, we need to continually realize (make real) how we are linked to the center and how our awareness grows for living there. In deep and crucial ways, the work of heart and mind is to stand by the center of life (accessed most intimately through the center of one's own life), and the work of consciousness is to listen to what that ever-present center continually says, though it may speak in languages other than the ones we are used to. The ancient Tao can be understood in these terms. Our ongoing work is to stand by the Tao, that mystical current of life, as we would a mountain stream in spring and to drink from it, not just to sustain our bodies, but as a way to imbibe its ways. Till we think and move like a mountain stream.

If Peace Is the Pool, Then Feelings Are the Fish

It is a constant challenge to find our center, our core, and to stay there long enough to uncover our capacities. Both require a steady movement inward. Yet all the while we are asked to face all that is disheartening along the way. For, if unfaced, disheartenment can fester and cause a virus in the eye that will blind us to what is central. Through the infected veil of disheartenment, we can step right over all that might sustain us. This is not to say that we must always be cheery. It is unprocessed feeling that feeds disheartenment. Feelings faced, in time, discharge disheartenment. So standing by one's core is not combative, but more about seeking peace by facing our experience, letting our feelings in, embracing our difficulties, and surrendering our useless notions of will—all without losing our self.

We often think that peace is the place we arrive at once we've dealt with our feelings or even rid ourselves of them. The assumption under this is that feelings are troublesome things that stand in the way of our peace. My experience has treated me differently. For try as I have for over fifty years to deal and rid myself of troubles, it's never worked that way. More often, facing my feelings, which is sometimes different than dealing with them, reduces them to a common element that I briefly know as peace. Though the things I feel will flare and transmute, I am rarely rid of them.

As such, I have known peace as the steady center that holds all my feelings. Though it seems paradoxical, when I am peaceful, I find myself in a center tantamount to the eye of a storm, from which I am free to feel all my feelings, singly and together, without any one taking over my life.

A Journey Toward Three Virtues

More than once I have encountered what I thought was failure, only to realize later that had I been given what I asked for, it would have buried my soul—with work that wasn't really mine, with upholding relationships that were never what I thought they were, with loyalties to maps bequeathed to me by lonely dreamers who wanted me to find what they could never find. And for a loving person, I must confess I have had a lot of relationships fail. Of course, over a lifetime, relationships will fail or run their course. But still, as I walk on yet another morning shore, watching the gulls fight and ride the early wind, I can't help but wonder, was it me?

I think, in most cases, I was standing by my core, finding myself inevitably in a place where loving on the terms required began to violate and damage that core. But I suppose those beautiful souls I was drawn to love thought they were standing by their core. And what if both are true? Is this another paradox about heartache to bare and bear? Is this all part of the inevitable journey toward the brutally exquisite fact of being here?

The great sociologist Robert Bellah outlines a journey toward three virtues that his friend Erik Erikson profoundly uncovered:

According to Erik Erikson, the problem of adolescence is the establishment of identity, and the good outcome is expressed in the virtue of fidelity; *the problem of adulthood is attaining the capacity to take responsibility for others as well as for oneself, and the good outcome is expressed in* the virtue of care; *the problem of old age is to find meaning in the whole of life in the face of one's own immanent death, and the good outcome is expressed in* the virtue of wisdom. *Of course these problems and virtues are inherent throughout one's life; they only become relatively prominent at particular points in the life cycle. There are wise children and old people who have never established their identity and many who in their whole lives have never learned to take care of others.*

Here, adolescence, adulthood, and old age are not defined outwardly in terms of years, but more as places on the way to living near the center. And so the ultimate aim of courage becomes a lifelong quest to know who we are, to care, and to find meaning in the face of death.

While thinking on all of this, I heard an architect say that a contemplative building is not one built for meditating, though meditation may take place there, but more a building where the inside is larger than the outside. It made me realize that anything that does this, that makes the inside larger than the outside, leads us to our core. And breathing there gives us peace. Now I

The Heart of It

And there, in the half-light,
the one song beneath our names
kept the last note in the air longer
and the night opened and without
a word, we loved each other . . .

Earlier, we considered the nature of a flute as a metaphor for how experience carves its holes in us, all for the chance to have the breath of life pass through us and make music in the world. Each being on earth is worn to such a flute, releasing our unique song of spirit through the holes carved by our experience.

Since stumbling on this notion, I haven't been able to stop thinking about flutes, even dreaming about them. And just today, I woke with an image of prehistoric beings carving holes in bones, trying to release their music. It sent me searching for the beginning of flutes. To my amazement, I found that three carved bones are among the oldest known musical instruments: a flute dated 37,000 years ago, made from the long curved tusk of a Russian mammoth, found in the Swabian Alb in Germany, a plateau rising toward the higher mountains of the Black Forest; a seven-hole flute, dated 36,000 years ago, made from a swan's bone, found in the Geissenklosterle Cave in Germany; and another dated about 50,000 years ago, made from the bone of a juvenile cave bear, found in Slovenia.

Given the rigors of their existence, what made these prehistoric beings devote so much time and energy to carving holes in animal bones? What made them first dream that breathing through the carved out bones would release music? It hardly seems practical or useful. Yet that they did, affirms that, even then, there was more to life than gathering sticks and cooking food. Even then, we had some intuitive image of how experience carves us and plays us, if we can only endure and listen.

Along the way, many of the wise have spoken to the carving of holes and the releasing of music. It was Thoreau who said, "The cost of a thing is the amount of what I call life which is required to be exchanged for it, immediately or in the long run." Doesn't he speak to the cost of being carved open? And earlier, St. Augustine said, "We come to God by love, not by navigation." Doesn't he speak to the breath of life rising through our wounds once we can surrender? Don't these two instructions lead us to each other? Isn't the cost of experience the amount of life given up in order to go on? And isn't the way to God beyond all compass work, in the wearing down of our will into the acceptance of love?

It seems the heart of it is to find the flute we each are hiding, carrying, being carved into. And hearing the music of life pass through our wounds and openings is how facing each other can make every stranger known. I wish I could have known the heart of that speechless pilgrim who carved the seventh hole in the bone of a swan 36,000 years ago. Somehow, I know we are the same. For experience is the best principle. Listening is the best way of knowing. Involvement is the best persuasion. Compassion is the best way of interpreting suffering. And love, the music rising from every human flute, is the best way to decipher the meaning of life.

God of the Broken Tusk

Pursue the obstacle . . . It will set you free.

Ganesh is the Hindu god who is the provider and remover of obstacles. He is typically depicted as an elephant. Ganesh is the lord (*Isha*) of all existing beings (*Gana*). Legend has it that when given the task to race around the universe, Ganesh did not traverse the outer surface of the earth, but simply walked *inwardly* around Shiva and Parvati, his mother and father, who are the source and center of all existence. This is the secret understanding of Ganesh as the provider and remover of obstacles. For all too often, the obstacles that we experience are presented as ways to remember that *the inner walk around the source*, not the outer race, is the purpose of living. The obstacles are presented to break our trance with the race and jar us humbly back to the source, and they are often removed once our deeper sense has been restored.

In Buddhism, *prajna garba* means *the womb of wisdom*, which implies that wisdom must be brought full term and given birth to. It seems the truth of experience can only release its wisdom if embodied. One chief way that embodied wisdom is brought full term is through the life of obstacles. We in the West, with our obsession to problem solve, have stubbornly made a devotion of *eliminating* obstacles—a devotion that often avoids *relating* to obstacles and staying in conversation with them. But, as older traditions confirm, it is the very journey *through* the life of obstacles that is the labor we must endure in order to birth any wisdom at all.

Living Through the World

It is important to realize that Ganesh is a god of *embodied* wisdom who knows the life of obstacles of which he is guardian. He is a god because he has *lived through* all the world has to offer, not because he transcends it. Often, he holds in his right hand one of his own tusks, which he broke off in a fit of anger and hurled at the moon. But the moon spit it back, and he carries that broken piece of himself as a reminder of the earthly journey that no one can escape.

Being jarred from the race around the universe, laboring through obstacles to birth wisdom, and carrying the broken pieces of ourselves as reminders of our humanity—these features of experience invoke a different relationship to things that get in the way. Often, the student in us works the problem, while our inner teacher is asking us to see things differently. Our problem-solving self is often frustrated by our inner teacher who says, "Are you sure this is a problem?" Waiting within all experience, Ganesh is the *God of the Broken Tusk* who lives between worlds. Ganesh is the teacher of teachers.

In his very personal book *Let Your Life Speak*, Parker Palmer suggests that if you turn around when a door closes, the whole world opens. But so often we just hang around the closed door. What keeps us there while the whole world waits? In our stubbornness, we begin to create our own obstacles and must wonder, what do they want to teach us? Two of the most stubborn inner obstacles are disappointment and failure.

Oddly, disappointment is defined by whether what happens is close or not to what we expect. We hear ourselves uttering, "That was disappointing" as opposed to "That was a surprise." Here, the inner obstacle is really our quick and endless dowry of expectations, which we create and then feel entitled to. As fast as we can think, we create pictures of what we want and where we want to be and how we want to be seen, then hold them out ahead of us as some strange form of gold we must have. Expecting life to conform to these images is a perversion of having a goal. It often prevents us from seeing what life freshly brings us.

Failure, it seems, is disappointment allowed to root within one's self-esteem. Yet after falling down enough, after having things pass through our hands repeatedly, after having so many of life's blessings arrive from beyond the range of all our schemes and plans, it seems odd to define success or failure by whether we get what we want or by how close we land to where we aim. Quite the contrary, failure would seem to be the limitations that cap our possibilities if we get *only* what we want and if we touch *only* what we aim for.

For example, not one of the books I've written—including this one—is the book I started out to write. Likewise, none of the people I've loved are those I set out to have a relationship with. And very few of the things I've learned are things I set out to learn. Nor did I have any idea that the things that have changed me from within were waiting to grow once what had covered them had been broken.

Without Ringing the Bell

More often than not, the deeper problem in meeting the life of obstacles is our understandable reluctance to work with what we are given. If we can get past our shattered expectations and recover from throwing our broken tusks at the moon, we have the chance to see what has unfolded as not less than we had hoped for, just different. If we can get this far, we can enter. Let me describe two examples.

My friend Joe had a cat, Russé, who was an exceptional hunter. Too good. So Joe put a bell around her neck so she would make noise, warning all the mice and chipmunks she would stalk. It was a designed limitation. But to his amazement, Russé only learned how to be *more* agile, *moving without ringing the bell at all!* What was first experienced as a limitation was the circumstance by which mastery was achieved. This is an exquisite example of Ganesh at work. The question and challenge for us is: how can we, in the midst of life's hardships, turn our woundedness and limitations into aliveness and mastery? How can we find Russé's freedom within the bells we find ourselves collared in?

Our second example involves the legendary violinist Itzhak Perlman. Jack Riemer of the *Houston Chronicle* tells the story of Perlman slowly moving his polio-stricken legs onstage at Lincoln Center in the fall of 1995. Once the music began, he was light as a bird—and then a string popped. There was a stunned silence. Riemer recounts what happened next:

Of course, anyone knows that it is impossible to play a symphonic work with just three strings. But that night, Itzhak Perlman refused to know that. You could see him modulating, changing, recomposing the piece in his head. At one point, it sounded like he was de-tuning the strings to get new sounds from them that they had never made before.

Afterwards, the heaviness of his legs returned to his body. Later, Perlman said, "You know, sometimes it is the artist's task to find out how much music you can still make with what you have left."

The point where woundedness sometimes turns to aliveness is ironically not where we assert our will, but where we learn to surrender and accept our limitations as doorways through which our mastery waits.

Somehow, Russé in her catness accepted the bell on her neck as a parameter within which she could find her agility. So rather than fight that boundary or limitation, she surrendered to it and discovered that she could master yet another level of movement *within* what made the bell ring.

This doesn't always work. Sometimes limitations are just that, limiting. But often, what we consider limiting merely focuses our abilities, if we surrender to it. In Itzhak Perlman's case, the string breaking on his violin caused him to surrender and focus on the strings that were left and a new field of music opened itself *inside* what was initially thought a constraint.

This is how some people in the midst of great illness or hardship find their threshold to God. How Monet could paint his water lilies as cataracts covered his eyes, how a deaf Beethoven could compose his astonishing ninth symphony, how a blind Milton could dictate *Paradise Lost* to his daughter.

The difference between limitation and threshold often hinges on whether we use our will to fight against the great forces that have, in an instant, already changed us or whether we use our efforts to discover our connection to everything through what is left, using that as a new form of instrument to be played. Often, the difference between enduring and transforming is the moment of surrender to this raw and new knowledge.

God's Timing

So living through our expectations, we begin to see that obstacles, like it or not, take us out of the comfort of what we know. They force us to grow. By breaking our enshrined sense of the future, the life of obstacles brings us back to the beginning. And being broken back to the beginning is how we find our way to God. We could say that another name for Ganesh is "God's Timing."

There is no question: working with limitations is humbling, but revealing. When the lip is cut, no matter how, the need to heal makes us chew slower and drink to one side. It makes us speak only when we have something to say. These are not bad things. When the mind is cut, by a truth too sharp to hold, it makes us bleed the things we cling to. If lucky, we bleed the things that no longer work. When the self others have sealed us in is cut, it lets us escape with only what we were given at birth.

In truth, while there are terrible ways to be opened, there is no such thing as a bad opening. It's all about God's timing. Not open enough and we fester. Open too long and we become a wound. Amazingly, if you speed up how a flower blooms, it appears to be escaping. If you slow down the way a crisis explodes what we know, it appears we are transforming. Hard as it is to embrace, crises are flowers opening what we refuse to open by ourselves.

Fighting the Instrument

All this has led me to view God as the sculptor and experience as His chisel. And try as we might to shape the things around us, it is *we* who are being sculpted. Since my eyes have been chipped open, I see things differently. Often the instruments of change are not kind or just, and the hardest openness of all might be to embrace the change while not wasting our heart fighting the instrument. The storm is not as important as the path it opens, the mistreatment in one life never as crucial as the clearing it makes in our heart. This is very difficult to accept. The hammer or cruel one is always short lived compared to the jewel in the center of the stone.

The Heart's Blossom

Courage is the heart's blossom.
It is the song from within
that keeps the pain of living
from snuffing our lives, the
way that fire stalls the cold.

All courage is threshold crossing. Often there is a choice—to enter the burning building or not, to speak the truth or not, to stand before oneself without illusion or not. But there is another sort of courage we are talking about here—the kind that, afterwards, the courageous are puzzled to be singled out as brave. They often say, "I had no choice. I *had* to run in that building for that child." Or "I *had* to quit my job, or I would have died."

Despite all consequence, there is an inevitable honoring of what is true, and at this deep level of inner voice, it is not a summoning of will, but a following of true knowing. My own life is a trail of such following. Time and again, I have heard deep callings that felt inevitable, which I could have ignored, but only at great risk of something essential perishing.

It was this honoring of what is true that guided me through my cancer experience—saying no to brain surgery and yes to rib surgery, saying yes to chemo and no to chemo. Each decision appeared both courageous and illogical to my doctors. And since then I have been called heroic for surviving, which is like championing an eagle for finding its nest, and I have been condemned as selfish for seeking the Truth, which is like blaming a turtle for finding the deep. Courage of this sort is the *result* of being authentic, of living what we know. It is available to all, and its reward, far more than respect, is the opening of joy.

Embodied Wisdom

Last summer, I had the good fortune to visit Naropa University in Boulder, Colorado. I have long known of Naropa and its good work, though I never knew where the name came from. Last summer, I heard the story. It seems that Naropa was an eleventh-century religious scholar in India, renowned for his complete mastery of all the forms and histories of Buddhism. One day, while walking through town, he met an old hag who piercingly asked, "Do you know the heart of these teachings?" Her abrupt question stopped the learned scholar, but he said, "Yes, of course." She came closer and peered right through his heart. She could tell he was lying. The old woman shook her head and walked away. When she was almost out of view, Naropa ran after her and asked that she be his teacher. Ever since, Naropa has been a symbol of the quest for embodied wisdom.

There are many inspiring models of embodied wisdom and many more we'll never hear of. Let me mention a few who cause me to marvel at their complete fidelity in following their true knowing, because to do otherwise, it seems, would have meant some form of inner death.

In Elizabethan times, Henry VIII demanded that all his subjects take an oath declaring that he was the supreme head of the

Church of England. In effect, this meant that he had primacy over the pope. This also would enable him to divorce his second wife, Anne Boleyn, for not siring a son. Sir Thomas More could not place Henry above God. He refused to obey the king's command, saying that when a man takes an oath, he holds his soul like water in his hands. If he should break that oath, his life would part, and his soul would slip through his fingers forever. Sir Thomas refused the oath because he knew he could not keep it. He knew, in pretending, he would lose his soul. In the end, he was beheaded in 1535 as an example, and his wife never forgave him for not signing what she called a silly piece of paper.

In the next generation, in Italy, the famous astronomer Galileo was put on trial in 1633 for heresy and threatened with death by the Roman Catholic Church unless he would recant his discovery that the earth wasn't the center of the universe. Eventually, he did recant, and his life was spared; though his writings were banned, and he lived the rest of his life under house arrest at Arcetri near Florence. It was there that he secretly wrote his masterwork, *Two New Sciences*, which greatly influenced both Isaac Newton and Albert Einstein. When I think of both More and Galileo, it seems clear that courage that stands by what we know at heart is not about pronouncing or denouncing, but something deeper than our words or our silence.

In Communist Russia, the great writer Aleksandr Solzhenitsyn was arrested in 1945 by the Soviet police for criticizing Joseph Stalin in a letter to a friend. Solzhenitsyn was sent to prison, where he was disrobed and set before a firing squad. The rifles fired blanks. The government was trying to psychologically kill him, to damage his voice. But it failed. Later, in a special labor camp in Ekibstuz, Kazakhstan, Solzhenitsyn worked on his book-length poem *Prussian Nights*. He had no pen or paper and wasn't allowed to write in any way. But he would compose a few lines each day, carve them into his bar of soap and recite them over and over to himself. And each evening, in his daily shower, he would recite them one more time, as the shower wore the words away. After years of captivity, he had written the entire book on a bar of soap and memorized all of it as the soap vanished.

In December of 1955, it was another typical day of inequality in Montgomery, Alabama, when Rosa Parks, who worked at the Montgomery Fair Department Store, was ordered to give up her seat to a white man on the crowded Cleveland Avenue bus. In the famous moment that followed, she quietly refused and the civil rights movement in America was launched. Because, as she would later describe, she feared what giving up her seat would do to her more than what would happen if she disobeyed. Sometimes we stand taller by not standing at all, but by refusing to give up what little we have.

And when two white guards beat Nelson Mandela daily in the prison yard of Robben Island off the coast of South Africa, he began to sing. On the fourteenth day, they stopped to ask him, "How can you sing?" He winced and smiled, saying, "Because my spirit is not my body." From that day forward, the guards would pretend they were beating him. To the surprise of thousands, Mandela called them up at his inauguration in 1994 as president, put his arms around them, and said, "These men are my friends."

Acts of courage like these are not planned or decided, but the result of obeying some compelling, inner clarity. They seem great only in retrospect. In the moment before they happen, they simply seem necessary in order not to have your soul slip like water through your fingers. As necessary as holding what you know close to you in silence. As simple and brave as carving words in a bar of soap. Or keeping your seat on a crowded bus. Or putting your arms around someone who has stopped hurting you.

Of course, that compelling inner sense is not always clear. Sometimes it seems very far away. I only know, for me, that when I can be the truth, it becomes more and more clear when it is necessary to tell the truth. That is, when I have access to the place within me that is lighted, I don't have to speak heatedly. I can just give away warmth. When I am still enough to brush quietly with eternity, I don't have to speak of God. I can just offer peace to those around me. I don't look to stand up for things, just to stand. Now I can see that a tree grows so it can convey wind. It is not the wind. And a person grows in order to convey spirit. They say that animals recharge their innocence each time they hoof the earth. And we are reborn each time we touch what matters.

A Sacred Becoming

Some are born as keys
looking for what they open.
And some are born as hidden
waterways searching for
what will open them.

So how do we encourage the heart to blossom? How do we go
about trying to embody wisdom? Through a sacred becoming.
When God is asked in the Torah for His name, a reply comes
from the unseeable, "I am Becoming . . . ." At once, *Becoming* em-
anates two meanings. As a noun, it suggests that God is a process,
that the sacred reveals itself in a life of transformation and unfolding. As a verb, it suggests that God is still emerging, still not
completely defined, beautifully as unfinished as we are. The story
implies that our unfolding and God's unfolding are intimately
entwined. You could say that the aim of any sacred becoming is
not to arrive at any finished state, but to taste everything in our
brush with life and thereby know, through experience, the hint
of what is holy.

The kind of courage this requires is both real and noble. Real
in the fact that the only way to "become" is through facing our
experience directly. And noble in what Parker Palmer calls "a
fidelity to the best potentials of the human spirit," staying faith-
ful to what is possible if we keep sparking tomorrow with who

we are today. The mystical Persian poet of the thirteenth century, 'Aṭṭār, who was an immediate ancestor to Rumi, endorses this kind of courage when he says, "For your Soul, seek Spiritual knowledge from what is Real."

In other words, though it is understandable to pray for God to remove us from our pain and confusion, God waits at the very heart of that pain and confusion, if we can "become" our way through it. This growing with God causes the heart to blossom. So it might serve us better to pray for the wherewithal to endure the flare of earthly moods that rims God's presence. For experience heats us through those earthly moods into what is central and sacred, the way that gold is melted at intense temperatures. It presses us into what is immediate and clear, the way that coal is pressed into a diamond. It wears us into what matters, the way the ocean wears the sharp edges from the mouth of a shell.

Yet how can we enter our "becoming" now, today? Especially in an age whose crosscurrents keep us on the surface? Our constant initiation is the call to go below that surface—no easy task. But in truth, any moment of experience will draw us below if we can ride it instead of fight it. And when asked, along the way, "What are you?" we can answer with Buddha, "I am Awake." When asked, as we fall and rise, "Who are you?" we can answer with Yahweh, "I am Becoming."

Movement 2

Being the Lion

Fires Looking for a Sea

From here
it deepens and the atoms
in my heart start to sing
and I am compelled
to voice things
I know nothing
about.

Eventually the art of being awake thins our protections until we are close to having nothing left between inner and outer. It leads us into the pain-joy of being alive with nothing in the way. There is less and less between heart and world. In the morning, I am sure this is a deep blessing. By night, it seems a curse. In time, our pains in being here crack open into a soft wonder that no one owns. I notice everything now, and more, I am everything I notice. Like one who suddenly sees while staring, I now know love, though I have been loving. In many ways, I'm not sure if I'm in trouble or on holy ground.

This has always been a holy, if confusing place. In the ancient Pali language of India, *citta* (*chitta*) refers to *the mind-heart*. But the word also indicates *a quality of motion, of fluctuation, a quivering* that characterizes how the mind-heart moves. The naming of citta as the mind-heart is like a snapshot, while the indication of its quivering quality is like a film of how the mind-heart stirs in its aliveness. This deep quivering place of citta describes the living center from which both aliveness and woundedness rise. It is here that events ripple through our very center, too forceful and whole to be sorted or silenced.

In her eighties, the playwright and Jungian analyst Florida Scott-Maxwell described what the juncture of aliveness and woundedness can feel like:

Some uncomprehended law holds us at a point of contradiction where we have no choice, where we do not always like what we love, where good and bad are inseparable partners impossible to tell apart, and where we—heart-broken and ecstatic—can only resolve the conflict by blindly taking it into our hearts.

It takes courage to blindly take the felt contradictions into our quivering center. It takes courage to live this thinly before the unpredictable roughness that storms about us on any given day. But risking less is just living in silhouette, all outline and no substance. It's hardly worth the trouble.

Last spring, I was in one of these holy, yet confusing moods, feeling inside out, with little protection. The wind itself seemed like a low flame. The past felt too near and the future too far away. I had wandered with some friends into a worn garden to hear an old cellist. Behind her was a waterfall, thin, steady, gentle, much like her. She was playing Bach, and slowly, I could feel the bow rubbing the strings, could feel her hand pushing the bow, could feel her heart pushing her hand, her eyes closed, drawing on the suffering and joy of a long life. And, opened like that, it occurred to me that the rubbing of strings until they produce music is as good a way as any to describe the thinning between inner and outer.

All my life I've tried to lessen what stands between my heart and the world, between my mind and the sky, between my eye and your eye. Never realizing that when who we are is our skin, well, yes, we can know the inside of mystery. We might even glimpse the face of God. But we also live like burn survivors screaming at the air. This too is part of being awake, this being on fire always looking for a sea.

This is why my wife cries at the deer sleeping in the snow. Why she wants to touch the flakes on their closed lids. The old cellist played before the waterfall, and everyone slouched, till somewhere inside, our hearts thinned like strings and our minds worked like bows. Ever since, I feel the living skin of heart laying itself bare before the draw and rub of beauty. We want so badly to be awake, never knowing the art that waits, when there is nowhere left to hide.

Aliveness and Woundedness

If you were to shield the canyons from the wind storms,
they would never show their beautiful carvings.
❖ *Elizabeth Kübler-Ross*

In Japan, traditional woodblock artists carve away what hides the
pattern to be printed. When it comes time to ink the board and
prepare the paper, the edges of paper are torn, not cleanly cut or
scissored. Why? Because, quite simply, the torn edge is considered more beautiful. In my heart, I know this to be so. In the tear
lies the beauty. It is a hard paradox we can never escape. And so
we must help each other make peace with it.

Experience rips us open. It carves away what hides the beauty.
I spent much of my youth running from this fact. But after cancer, I was walking among the ancient redwoods in California
with the dearest of friends, when he picked up a laurel leaf from
the forest floor and tore it open under my nose. A fragrance it
had held for centuries filled me. I knew from this broken open
leaf that all I'll ever write—all anyone can ever write or say—
will be such a fragrance rising from the places where life tears us
open or breaks us apart.

It's led me to wonder about aliveness and woundedness. It
doesn't seem possible, but the torn edge *is* more beautiful. I can
finally see it. And just as the mystery of air can only be entered
by inhabiting the rhythms of inhaling and exhaling, the fragility

of being here, uncovered by suffering, can only be entered by inhabiting the rhythms of aliveness and woundedness. Somewhere—inside each breath, inside each suffering—a wisdom waits, if we can enter and listen to the many ways that silence can sing.

Why Am I the Only One Crying?

I met a woman who has loved Mozart her whole life. We were at a large dinner party. She sat next to me and quietly said, "You know, I have a Jewish background, but I go sometimes to their church. It's so somber that it makes me cry. I've lost two teenage girls, you know. I look around and no one even moves. Their Lord died two thousand years ago. Why am I the only one crying?" She stared off past my salad and then offered, "It's why I love Mozart, because under all his skill, the one chord he returns to keeps saying, 'Why am I the only one crying?'"

Is this woundedness or aliveness? It is surely an example of having very little left between your heart and life. While some think this makes us weak, I believe it is what we are put here for: to wear away and love away everything in between. Much depends on what we do with such a sensibility. Clearly, carrying the weight of feeling and perception and having nowhere to go with it is the burden of being a watcher. It can be lonely and debilitating. But when we can give voice to and share what rises through us, it joins us. Ultimately, what we do with the waterfall of our sensitivities matters. That the woman who loves Mozart dared to break through her polite conversation with a stranger to speak of the tenderness of being alive keeps that unexpected feeling from festering into a wound. Between us, the feeling stays alive. Between us, the tenderness helps us live.

In truth, aliveness and woundedness are ever-changing states that we move through like wakefulness and sleep. And it seems that the practice of honest expression is necessary to move from sleep to wakefulness and from woundedness to aliveness. Being human, we are constantly slipping from one to the other. Repeatedly the cost of not expressing who we are turns out to be woundedness. Not surfacing who we are and what we feel results in self-echo, dividedness, isolation. If allowed to fester, wounds can't heal. Then we risk imploding. On the other side, the gifts of expressing who we are manifest in our aliveness. Such commitment to the flow of presence results in connection, wholeness, and membership in the Universal Ground of Being. And when everything comes alive, wounds given to air can heal. Then we risk falling in love with everything.

Before the Split

Our training to split what matters has a long history, and it seems inevitable that civilization's compulsion to dissect would lead us into a modern world that views splitting the atom as a triumph. If we go back, it seems the Renaissance mind became a filter that moved us away from a unified understanding of life and cleaved the way we think. For example, before the Renaissance split the word *daimon* into "good" angels and "bad" demons, the phrase in Greek meant *a divine spirit* and included both nourishing spirits as well as challenging ones, both muses and tricksters. And before the modern mind defined *brilliance* as the ease of uncanny skill, the word meant the emanation of being that was brilliant like the sun. Powerfully, *genius* was not reserved for Mozart or Einstein alone, but was originally a phrase that referred to *an attendant spirit*, or genie, if you will, a guardian angel that every person had access to.

Likewise, before the western mind regarded happiness as an inalienable right and therefore saw pain and sadness as unnatural psychic sediments to be rid of, aliveness and woundedness were viewed as aspects of life dependent on each other in order to access something deeper than happiness—joy. We can see this reflected in the ancient mythologies. Consider the *Chien*, the mythic bird of ancient China, an enormously colorful bird that has only one eye and one wing. It was believed that each Chien had to find another in order to see and fly. Similarly, though aliveness and woundedness are often perceived as separate and even antithetical, they are, in fact, crucial and complementary aspects of the same essential life force. Together they help us to see and fly.

I keep wondering about the notions of aliveness and woundedness and how they keep the heart. In deep ways, this book explores how aliveness and woundedness inform each other and how each, if viewed as separate, can trap us in self-destructive patterns that seem difficult to escape. When splitting up what matters and going it alone, we can fall into the crippling arc of tearing the wings off smaller things in replication of our pain. But when we dare to keep things whole and live together, aliveness and woundedness appear as inevitable wings which, working as one, can help us find each other.

Everything or Nothing

Sooner or later, we come to the edge
of a vastness that has been there all along
and we are forced to decide if we are
visitors or if this is our home.

We have countless opportunities to face the mystery of all that
is larger than us. Often, the winds of that threshold are strong
and painful, and whatever might bring us to that threshold—the
death of a loved one, a sudden loss of purpose, the loneliness of
success—we always have the choice whether to face what we
are opened to or not.

A touching story in this regard is of a young man living with
his parents in Baltimore while going to college. His father, a
quiet train conductor, came home one day and shot himself in
his son's room. The young man was devastated. There was no
explaining why his father had taken his life and, even more puz-
zling, why he chose to leave his bloody remains for his son to
find.

The young man struggled for months, depressed and undone.
Most of his friends couldn't walk the long walk with him. Many
stopped calling. One friend remained. It is through him that I
know what happened next.

The young man and his friend went to the Jersey shore for
a weekend, and, late that night, they sat for a long time on the

rocks listening to the sea. They talked about the pain and wonder of being alive, and the young man said, "I didn't ask to be here."

It was soon after this that his only friend felt a strange presence begin to open around them. He felt if they could just stay long enough, this presence mounting in the ocean might heal them. But just as he felt this presence opening, the troubled young man got up and left. On the way home, the young man, who kept seeing his father's remains in his room, confessed, "I felt the abyss opening up back there."

Afraid to say anything, his remaining friend tells me thirty years later that he was sure it was everything that was opening, not nothing, and that his sad friend had turned away from what was going to heal him. Of course, no one knows exactly what awaited them on that shore. And no one knows what it was like to be that poor young man. But the situation exemplifies how often we are on the verge of everything or nothing—or both. I'm not sure what became of him. But this is a story and a debate that has gone on for centuries. And which side of it we fall into will define our life.

On the Verge

It seems the closer we get to being broken open, the more rawly we experience the muscle of paradox. It is not so much that "every cloud has a silver lining," but more that inside everything that is breakable, including us, is the one unnamable thing that is *unbreakable*.

In his searing story of the Holocaust, Elie Wiesel tells of a bluish gray morning filled with despair, and the prevailing image was of a young boy hanging, his lifeless body swaying before dawn. A worn voice beside him uttered, "Where is God?" And Wiesel answered, "In the boy hanging . . ."

What can this mean? And how is it helpful? Let me speak to this with my own story. Three weeks after having a rib removed from my back, I went to New York City to receive my first chemo treatment, which was horribly botched. My former wife Ann and my old friend Paul came along to stand guard, unsure against what. We rented a room in a nearby Holiday Inn. Within an hour after the treatment, I began retching and vomiting every twenty minutes for the next twenty-four hours. Each time, the internal slash where they had taken out my rib grew more sore. We thought each episode would be the last. About four in the morning, I began spitting blood. We began to look for emergency rooms. At five, just before dawn, we were all slumped on the floor. I could barely speak. Through her tears, Ann grew angry and uttered the same question, "Where is God?" I don't know from where or from what, but I heard myself whisper, "Here. Right here."

It's as if what is unbreakable—the very pulse of life—waits for everything else to be torn away, and then in the bareness that only silence and suffering and great love can expose, it dares to speak through us and to us. It seems to say, if you want to last, hold on to nothing. If you want to know love, let in everything. If you want to feel the presence of everything, stop counting the things that break along the way.

These are extreme examples, but they point to a mood of depression that we all experience, some more stubbornly than others. In that mood, on the verge of all that matters, we pace the dark shore like that tragic young man from Baltimore. What we pick up at those moments can save us. The Jungian analyst Don Raiche describes this verge point well:

The chilling logic of depression will readily exterminate ourselves and most of the world, yet some small response of warmth—the heart refusing to deny the beauty or value of some part of ourselves or another being—can release and allow that warmth which, while easily snuffed, if sheltered may spread and with devotion and time melt the icy hold of the depression itself. The flickering image we shield may be of a loved one, a pet, a tree for which one delays the suicide saying, "No, there is this."

So, paradoxically, the journey to the edge of all-there-is is narrow at times. Even when the whole of life remains out of view, especially then, a slow courage is required to move through the eye of nothing into the galaxy of everything. To outwait nothing till the light of everything burns the grayness off and warms our thoughts like sunlight through a sheath of clouds. Sometimes it can take years. The legendary Carl Jung struggled terribly with depression and confusion as he wandered inwardly for eight years en route to his discovery of the collective unconscious. Looking back, he recalls:

Thus I suffered and was miserable, but it seems that life was never wanting and even in the blackest night, and just there, by the grace of God I could see a great light. Somewhere there seems to be great kindness in the abysmal darkness of the Deity.

We are all just guests in a body that comes and goes. When on the verge of leaving that body, it becomes clear that there is a flame in everything. If I look long enough, I can see the flicker in the meat of a tree, and just this morning I saw it in the slender throat of a doe nibbling through early mist. If still enough, I can hear the flame at the center of the earth, which nothing can contain. Yes, flowers are just licks of flame breaking through in spring.

It's the same in you and me, in every stranger afraid to speak, a small pilot light that no one can put out, and love and truth make it burn brighter and we call the brightness joy. But if you want to see the small living flame itself, well, that's strange business. It's somewhat like the stars—it's always there but only see-able in the dark. It's why the heart, when least expected, glows like a candle in each moment of despair.

The Fall into Life

If you love everything, you will perceive the Divine Mystery in
all things.

❖ *Fyodor Dostoyevsky*

At her fifty-ninth birthday party, a dear friend said, "For all I've
been through, I wouldn't trade the journey of being alive for
anything." To me, she is of a lineage that holds experience as
sacred, a lineage that implies a different interpretation of our relationship to Eden. The next day, I asked her about this, and, after
a long silence, she said, "It just might be that Adam and Eve felt
trapped in the sameness of Eden. Maybe they deliberately ate of
the tree of knowledge in order to be sent into the world. Maybe
they needed to know life fully, needing precisely the knowledge
of good and evil in order to experience meaning."

This suggests that a different myth governs our time on earth,
one that says we are intended to experience the fullness of life
through our interaction with *everything*—good and bad, joyous
and sad, peaceful and painful, full and empty. It suggests that,
more than a garden of purity existing outside of life, Eden is a
garden of humility that waits on the other side of suffering and
wonder, once we've been shaped by our tumble through time.

This all implies that our fall into life is inevitable and that
through this journey into what is real, we leave our idea of God
and meet God. Though no one wants to hear it, some will say

that Adam and Eve were afraid to venture into the world. That
the snake was a crippled angel born without wings. That God
promised to complete the snake, if it would lead the human
fledglings into the world where they belonged. But once eating of the Tree of Knowledge, Adam and Eve still refused to
leave, and, in spite of their refusal, God sent them on into their
destiny.

To remind them that they must always leave what is used up
behind, God sent His crippled angel into the world to slither
underfoot, giving it the ability to shed its skin. And this ability to
shed completed the snake. This ability to shed was its wings.

Imagine, Eden is a preparation, not a destination.

The Danger of Falling

Still, living from the quivering place and jumping into life has
its dangers. We can be thrown under when unable to make a
strength of our tenderness. We can even collapse. There is hardly
a more poignant example than the fire-burst of a painter, Vincent Van Gogh. Here was a tragic-heroic example of a human
spirit riding the edge between aliveness and woundedness. Here
was someone so sensitive that he had access to the sublime and
so sensitive that life broke him apart.

It was pure gift that Van Gogh could approach the inside of everything. In his painting *Wheat Fields with Cypresses* (June 1889),
the elements—earth, air, trees, clouds—become numinous and
indistinguishable, as they begin to reveal their common shimmer, an energy of pure motion that quantum physicists describe
a hundred years later as the unending movement that inhabits

everything. In late June of 1889, a month after his arrival at the asylum in Saint-Rémy and a month before his apparent suicide, Van Gogh wrote his brother Theo that he had twelve canvasses going at once. He was becoming a spiritual Icarus, feverishly painting the pure pulse of life—fire was like water and earth was all aflame. He was being drawn closer and closer to the sun, on his way to burning up.

I know of no way to safeguard against such pure heat taking over the soul. Yes, there are inner practices and the comfort of loved ones and friends to keep us tethered to the earth. There are many lessons of balance and equanimity from many traditions. But the truth is that it is just as dangerous to fly too close to the sun as it is to wither in the caves, never coming into the light. And humbly, unpredictably, the line between being Monet and Van Gogh is wispy at best. The line between being lighted and ebullient and dark and brooding is but a veil.

These are not abstract ideas, but paradoxes that can grip us tomorrow. When we isolate and watch from the shadows, we court a living death. When we immerse and try to eat the sun, we are consumed by flame. All the while, there is no meaning unless we engage life head on and heart on.

In 1987, an old friend traveled through India, and in his diary he heard this anonymous teaching along the way:

The sugar cane should welcome the cutting, the hacking, the crushing, the boiling and the straining to which it is subjected. Without these ordeals the cane would dry up and make no tongue sweet. So, too, must we welcome trouble for that alone gives sweetness to the spirit within.

It's true. Life can cut us, hack us, crush us, and boil us until we turn sweet. Yet for those of us awakened too softly to our quivering place, the strain can be too much. But the risk of withholding is that we may never know what it is to be alive. Still, waking and seeing and falling into life is illuminating *and* dangerous. And we all must find and honor the line between burning and burning up, between breaking open and breaking apart, between silencing our noise and losing our tongue. When I think of Van Gogh admitting himself to the asylum in Saint-Rémy a month before his suicide, I think of how we all need asylum of one kind or another.

I felt compelled to trace the word. I found that *asylum* is from the Middle English, meaning *refuge*, which in turn is derived from the Greek *asulon*, meaning *sanctuary*. But the most meaningful asylum is not a place in the world that we retreat to, but an inward pool of grace, a bottomless spring we must refind, cutting down all that has grown in the way since the last time we were there.

The Sound One

Can we guard against the danger of falling into the sun or freezing in the waters of the watcher's cave? Well, I don't know. There are many tools and many questions from many traditions. In Egyptian cosmology, the eye of the god Horus forms the sun. An early myth explains the sun's daily setting and rising as Horus' temporary loss and ultimate recovery of his central eye. The restored eye is known as "the Sound One." Imbedded in this myth is a process of hope. For the daily setting and rising of Horus represents our human cycle from turmoil to peace, our own recurring movement from darkness to light, and our spiral from confusion to clarity. This implies that being "sound" is the state of being restored on the other side of experience, seeing more clearly for having gone through encounters, not conquering or eliminating difficulties. The temporary loss and ultimate recovery of our central eye reflects the human process of wisdom. So being sound is not arriving at a disengaged halfway point from which we stay half engaged. Being sound has more the feel of whitewater rafting, working to stay in the center of the life-giving current that meanders swiftly through the smooth and jagged days.

How do we do this? Again, history is a storehouse of guesses. But one purpose of seeking knowledge is to navigate the rough waters between aliveness and woundedness. One approach is in Sufism. In that tradition, the Islamic word *'ilm* means *seeking knowledge*, and the purpose of knowledge centers on the notion of *tawhīd*, the effort to affirm and access the unity of God. In each person, this involves two sources of knowing, the outer knowing, *zāhir*, and the inner knowing, *bāṭin*. And the governing soul in each of us that merges inner and outer knowing—that which complements light with dark and dark with light, that which integrates—is a person's *adab*. This word is harder to translate. It refers to one's place of inner steering. You could say our adab is similar to our true self, equivalent with our restored central eye, with being "sound" enough to set and rise, like Horus, day after day.

One's adab or sound, true self is considered to be a living thing that we need to cultivate a relationship with. It is something crucial and inner, a seat of wisdom that we must stay in conversation with. Often, the health of this inner friendship and the clearness of that conversation determine if we experience meaning and how much time we spend in our aliveness or in our woundedness.

It's a never-ending practice, and the difference between feeling alive or wounded just might wait in the fiery edge between being lighted and burning up. Is it the fate of being human to live in between? Too close to the Source and we vanish in the heat. Too far away and we grow cold and fall asleep. Yet over a lifetime, we are used up anyway as the beautiful fuel of eternity. So, at best, a wise and long life may ask us to simply burn slowly so as to warm and light each other along the way.

Four in the Morning

Beauty is what's left
when all the illusions
are scoured away.

Often, making it to tomorrow requires standing in the fire without being burned. And that mysterious, yet difficult rite of passage requires some form of skin that is both porous and resilient—the skin of self-respect, of love, of truth, of compassion. These are the human skins that meet the world, that can keep us from being burned, though never from the joys and sorrows of feeling. For it seems that in order to fall into life, we must fall through darkness. And it is our joys and sorrows, undressing into something unnameable, that take us there.

It was St. John of the Cross, a sixteenth-century Spanish friar, who first referred to the Dark Night of the Soul. As a lonely explorer pauses to name a constellation when lost in the middle of the night, St. John named something that others have witnessed throughout time. We all encounter it. It's hard to describe, though its impact is unmistakable. It comes as a shattering passage when all we know is brought into question, when the ground of our assumptions and the brittle walls we've been relying on and hiding behind appear to be useless. Some call this a midlife crisis, or more deeply, an existential breach. In the world of addicts, it is known as hitting bottom. But whatever its color or flavor or timing, it marks the time in the growth of a life when we have the chance to drop below illusion into the Ultimate Reality that grounds all existence. Though it is inevitable and essential, it is never an easy passage.

Yet, after resisting enough, some of us surrender to the conclusion that being hatched and rearranged into a deeper form of living, though the journey be painful, is where we are all heading. In fact, the alternative seems far worse. Like the frog put in a pot of water which is brought slowly to a boil, the numb life of illusion slowly cooks us without our knowing. Better to be shattered of false ways and help each other heal anew. The Jewish thinker Leon Wieseltier puts it starkly:

There are circumstances that must shatter you; and if you are not shattered, then you have not understood your circumstances. In such circumstances, it is a failure for your heart not to break. And it is pointless to put up a fight, for a fight will blind you to the opportunity that has been presented by your misfortune. Do you wish to persevere pridefully in the old life? Of course you do: the old life was a good life. But it is no longer available to you. It has been carried away, irreversibly. So there is only one thing to be done. Transformation must be met with transformation. Where there was the old life, let there be the new life. Do not persevere. Dignify the shock. Sink, so as to rise.

Still, many of us dangle painfully on the edge of first light, unable to go back and unable to move through our Dark Night. Sadly, we take up residence there. In this painful position, the mind eats itself with worry and unworthiness, replaying confusion upon confusion, reliving wound after wound. I have lived there at times. The Taoist philosopher Chuang Tzu (c. 275 B.C.) describes that place of dark agitation this way:

To wear out one's intellect in an obstinate adherence to the individuality of things, not recognizing the fact that all things are one—this is called Three in the Morning.

Three in the Morning refers to a parable which exposes inconsequential knowing. We all fall prey to *Three in the Morning Mind.* It is part of what the Dark Night feels like.

In contrast to this, I was part of a retreat centered on generosity of spirit, in which ancient stories from around the world were read and discussed. The first night, the stories and the kind souls gathered there drew me to reread Chuang Tzu, and I realized that when we can outlast our agitation and feel the fact that all things are one, then we quite naturally care for the unseeable threads that connect us in a timeless practice known as generosity. And this we can call *Four in the Morning.* It is that mysterious hour of darkness—between three and four—in the middle of our night that holds the seed of our human journey.

Uncannily, by the third day of the retreat, our first guest had to leave at four in the morning to catch her plane. And quietly, five of her new friends rose in the middle of the night to walk her to the airport van. Without a word, these strangers were being generous to each other. This simple, unexpected effort to accompany each other through the dark moved me greatly. They were defining *Four in the Morning Heart.*

It became clear that when blessed to help each other live through that dark hour, we can move from inconsequential knowing to indispensable knowing, from believing things are separate to recognizing that all things are one. In that mysterious but bare realization, we can undress a stubborn mind into an open heart. Facing this unnameable hour between three and four is what prefigures dawn in the human heart. In deep ways, it is the purpose of a life to cross that one hour in between.

Between the Tiger and the Dragon

As coal under great pressure turns into a diamond, our spirit under great pressure has the chance to turn into the jewel that it is. This has always been known.

There is an old Sufi story that has a man leaving one life for another, and far enough into the desert that he has no sense of where he has been or where he is going, he senses a wild tiger chasing him. He has nowhere to go. Frantically, he runs and runs and comes upon a well. As the tiger approaches, he has no choice but to jump into the dark well. As he falls, he can see the tiger growling above him. As he falls, he can suddenly see that a dragon is hissing and waiting for him at the bottom of the well. Just then, he sees a branch growing out of a stone in the well. He grabs it. Amazingly, it holds his weight. As he strains to hold on, with the tiger above and the dragon below, a single ray of light falls on the one leaf on the one branch that holds his life. And on that leaf, in the light, is a single drop of honey. With the hissing of the dragon and the growling of the tiger in his ears, the man, leaving one life for another, summons all his strength, to lick the single drop of lighted honey. The story ends there with the man, en route to a new life, savoring the single drop of honey while the tiger and the dragon wait.

The power of this ancient story is that it affirms that spirit and crisis work each other in the world, and that the Divine Source is at the heart of every moment, even in the midst of danger. Mysteriously, the way that pressure makes the diamond hidden in a piece of coal visible, the press of the tiger and the dragon makes the essence in the moment visible. It makes the essence of who we are visible. Again and again, we are shown, though it is hard to accept, that life is a jewel waiting in each moment broken open. Whatever the tiger, whatever the dragon, the drop of lighted honey, once seen and tasted, can bless us. And licking that drop of lighted honey is what life is all about. It may not save us from suffering or even death, but it will let the spirit become the jewel that it is. It will let us experience radiance.

For me, one drastic meeting of the tiger and the dragon was during my cancer experience, when I was caught between the tiger of cancer and the dragon of chemo. I was afraid of cancer chasing me and terrified to continue with the treatment. There, like the Sufi wanderer, I was forced to jump into the dark well, and the single branch appeared. Briefly, I could feel the safety of that simple, eternal moment holding me up. While everything was coming apart, this moment was not the suffering in pursuit of me nor the fear of where the treatment might lead. Ever so briefly, I held onto the branch, and yes, it was lighted from somewhere beyond me—that is, its light was not dependent on me.

It was then I saw clearly. As I gambled on the future, I knew that the lighted moment with all its promise was intact. It was not up for grabs. I knew that this lighted branch of a moment, for which I'd lived all others, for which I'd withstood the breakage of all I know repeatedly, this moment was germ-free and not on trial. And so I summoned all my strength to say to my doctors, "You are welcome here by permission only and the alarm you cast will only snag my want for tomorrow, only hook what I do not have." I said with unexpected calm, "I know you mean to help, and I cannot deny you are a bridge I have to cross. But where I live cannot be staged or stained or seen as gross evidence. Where I live, where I've arrived is impervious to histology. It is the one site in the city that will not burn. And if you guide me to tomorrow, I'll show you, as you shake your head, how I still glow in this unbreachable clearing that I carry with me like a honeyed leaf lighted by the sun."

Blessed to still be here, I am only concerned with carrying that lighted moment everywhere I go, and when I lose it or drop it, my only concern is to find it between the tiger and the dragon, no matter what form they take today. And a strange truth has risen from all this: that when we are one with our gift, in that moment we are protected, not from suffering, but from the terror of life without honey or light. Thus, as the writer Lewis Hyde says, "It is your task to set free your gift." Not just to move goodness further into the world, but as a way to find the branch that holds the honey in the well between the tiger and the dragon.

This requires courage. It requires standing by one's core in the face of danger and the press of life. Specifically, this requires the courage to look through our fear. For while running from a tiger, while falling down a well, ever closer to the dragon at the bottom, our fear, understandably, blinds our ability to see. Yet the branch is always there, often unnoticed within the storm of our fear. There's no blame in this. It's just a fact of emotional physics. This is why all the meditative practices prepare us to find the still point in the storm. For seeing from there is our way to the next moment.

An anonymous poem from the fourteenth century in Japan captures this ageless instruction, when it says:

All tempest has,
like a navel,
a hole in its middle
through which
a gull can fly
in silence . . .

It is this moment within the storm, within our fear, that enables us to see the branch waiting between the tiger and the dragon. It makes perfect spiritual sense. In fact, artists have always been compelled, consciously or not, to search for the stillness in the storm and the honey in the well; always trying to pull themselves out of crisis by finding and riding the force of life itself. It is a lesson for us all. Willa Cather, in her novel *Song of the Lark*, evokes this sense poignantly:

What was any art but a mold in which to imprison for a moment the shining, elusive element which is life itself—life hurrying past us and running away, too strong to stop, too sweet to lose.

In truth, we are all instruments of an elemental art: our lives the brush, our expressions the color, our days the canvas. And by trying to find and ride the force of life itself, we search out the shimmering, elusive element that Cather speaks of, which, when found and tasted, keeps the tiger and the dragon at bay—the way the flicker of a candle keeps the dark from consuming it. The courage lies in finding the honey wherever it might be, within or without, and feeding it to each other, even to the tiger and the dragon.

What Gets in the Way

Something we were withholding made us weak
Until we found out that it was ourselves.
❖ Robert Frost

It's hard to describe what gets in the way. We can point to blind spots in our consciousness, or the stubbornness of our secret forms of greed, or the alarm of our exaggerated fears. But what gets in the way of honest living is as pervasive and invisible as air or wind or time. Because it encircles us, it's hard to see. Still, it helps to look. I remain convinced that finding the courage to face things as they are and to own our part in all that we trample is an inborn, if seldom used, gift that can diminish how we suffer. Otherwise, we become walking afflictions.

Just what keeps us, then, from knowing in our bones that everything is irreplaceable and teeming with Spirit? And how do our habits and fears mute our firsthand experience? Unto themselves, they are just debris cast about by the blinding storm. So let's focus instead on the conditions that give rise to the storm.

Three Forms of Work

If chickens don't get enough light, they start pecking at each other. The truth is that humans are no different. Once the pecking begins, we are called to three forms of work: stop the pecking, heal the wounds, and seek out more light. The eternal squabble has always been which of these efforts comes first: governance and law, medical and social healing, or education. Of course, an enlightened community does all three, but the deeper question is what combination will provide a lasting solution.

We won't solve that debate here, but the same dynamics confront us as individuals, alone and together. The removal of light causes us to peck at ourselves and each other. Ironically, the more removed we are from light, the less faith we have in its restorative powers. Until all our energy is spent strategizing how to peck or how to avoid being pecked. Then, the first task for any newcomer, regardless of their community, is to learn the pecking order.

Before farmers realized it was a lack of light that prompted all this pecking, we thought it was due to the nature of chickens, that they were loners who couldn't mingle without being nasty. In some quarters, their beaks were clipped, but this only made it more difficult for the chickens to eat. It only made them hungrier, until hunger and lack of light made them peck at each other even more. The parallels are obvious. Profoundly, it's not the free range of our thinking and the depth of our feelings that are dangerous, but that our minds and hearts are often incubated in the dark. We just need to hold each other more fully in the light.

The Thing about Darkness

Having made far too many decisions while in pain, having wasted too much energy trying to avoid pain, having spent lifetimes reaching for love in the dark, I want to share what I've begun to see. There is this thing about darkness. Let me try to explain. When I am closest to the earth, often after a fall, I somehow know that the side of God's face that goes dark does so the way the moon goes dark because *we*, like the earth, turn away. It's how most things go dark—not because they are dark, but because we can't or won't turn with them as they follow the light. It is we who seldom own the distance we create. It is this distance that often creates darkness. And evil arises when those who resist the inevitable pull into life make an enemy of all that they have distanced themselves from. These are aspects of human weather, and we do better to become students of these patterns than to engage life as an enemy.

Relentless Building

Ecologists and civil engineers are discovering that a disturbing byproduct of urban sprawl is how the relentless building of roads, parking lots, malls, and condominiums is literally sealing off vast surfaces of the earth. Over time, we are learning that this is preventing rain from seeping naturally into the earth where it nourishes root systems and replenishes underground aquifers. The importance of this is that without water to feed root systems, the healthy magic of spring is stunted. When the rain can't replenish the aquifers, then rivers and streams cease to be fed, which chokes the life cycle of fish, which interrupts the natural food chain.

Furthermore, when the rain can't penetrate the concrete lining we are building, it has to go somewhere, and so it floods.

Given this, we are seeing an increase in resources being spent to control flooding, which only diverts the much-needed water further away from the very land that needs it in the first place. In systems theory, this form of thinking is known as a *doom-loop*.

There is a startling parallel here to how we seal over the deeper nature of our experience. The modern sprawl of noise and consumerism is forming an impenetrable lining of culture that diverts our experience from seeping naturally into the ground of our being. Our modern obsession with doing, buying, having, with makeovers, fame, and celebrity, is creating a form of spiritual drought. Covering the earth with our diversions prevents experience from watering our roots. Then, when plain living has no way to enter us, it floods, and we start to believe that it's the experience of living that can't be managed or trusted. And so we avoid life more, diving further into our diversions, which are the problem in the first place. It's a damning cycle, *a perceptual doom-loop*.

Undoing the seal of our culture is an overwhelming task, but we can begin by saving our own lives, by putting down what linings we carry or wear, by letting our skin again be our skin, by restoring direct experience and letting the air and rain hit our lips.

Being Partial

We could say there is a correlation between the rise of the assembly line and the increase in the modern era of depression and alienation. We could say that when people cease to have the chance to work on the Whole, they lose contact with the

Whole. Thus, depression and alienation are made worse by the malnutrition of being partial. So what if it's more efficient to have one person put the second hand on a thousand clocks a day. Is it worth it if they never get to assemble time themselves? This is how specialization has ruined us. In doing partial work, we suffer being partial.

We must consider, then, the work we are given and asked to do. Is it the work we need in order to be whole? Is it the work we need in order stay in contact with things larger than us? Clearly, the faster we go, the more partial things get. The slower we go, the more present we are, and the more present we are, the more we experience the Whole. So be generous to your self and look for work and play that makes you feel complete.

Of course, we can't always find work that will keep us whole and pay the bills. Our only recourse then is to *not* define ourselves by what we have to do to eat. While preserving who we are, we have to tend to our inner hunger any way we can. It is as imperative as feeding a starving child. For the soul can starve, too.

Relentless Hunger
As soon as we covet what someone else is or has,
that desire prevents us from seeing what *we* have.
⋄ *Paul Bowler*

I was at a conference, and in the basement of the enormous hotel was a casino. Having only been once or twice, I was curious. As I entered the windowless room, I was stopped right away by the sight of a woman working two slot machines at once. I learned that she had been there all day, never leaving for fear that the moment she would leave, the jackpot would flood from the mouth of the machine and she would miss it. This painful scene struck me as a metaphor for that part of us that always looks for life other than where we are. Whether our search is for wealth or love or success in the eyes of others, the underlying sense that life is not where we are, but always just out of reach, cripples us. It enervates our will to live by siphoning our best efforts into entanglements that are difficult to escape.

I think our current problem with obesity is a painful form of gambling, which presupposes that if we take enough in, the right one will relieve us of our relentless hunger. The painful truth is that so many of us keep eating things that are ultimately unfulfilling, and so we never satisfy our hungers. Carl Jung described alcoholism as an attempt to quench a spiritual thirst with the wrong drink. Similarly, our obsession with eating seems an attempt to feel full by ingesting the wrong foods. What we really need is to empty ourselves in order to feel at all.

I recently went through my own bout with eating. Over a period of four years, I became overweight without realizing it. My knees began to hurt. My energy became heavy. I began to feel like I was moving underwater. With my wife Susan's help, I've managed to lose thirty-five pounds, and, more than feeling physically renewed and so much lighter, I feel clear again—as if waking from a subtle form of amnesia. Now I have regained the distinction between cravings and hunger, which I didn't know I'd lost. Now I have immense compassion for anyone trying to break the cycle of relentless hunger. For no one sets out to eat too much or drink too much or spend too much. No one aims to lose themselves.

A Deeper Response

It is as true as it is old: feed the inner hunger and the outer hunger will dissipate. Ignore the inner hunger and nothing in the world will satisfy you. So many things get in the way, not because life is out to trap us, but because the journey through it all is how a spirit awakens in a body on earth. And we are challenged to dig for a deeper response. When you catch yourself pecking, look for more light. When you find yourself darkened by pain, wait until you can see. When life seems to flood you, put down your mask. When feeling cut off and depressed, look for work that is whole. And when feeling you will die if a particular hunger is not fed, let that part of you die. Get out of your own way.

Near Enemies

Looking through water can make sharp edges seem soft, the way looking through what we want can make what is dangerous seem friendly.

In Buddhism, *near enemies* describes traits and efforts that look like earnest steps toward right being and right action, but that are actually counterfeit enticements, which, in the end, only derail and deflate us. For instance, the near enemy of true selflessness might be an obsession with self-sacrifice in order to be regarded as having no self. The near enemy of true compassion might be pity, which brings us close without feeling the other. The near enemy of true patience might be hiding. And the near enemy of acceptance might be tolerance. Consider that the near enemy of unconditional love might be the temptation of sweetened conditions, which, in the end, incur some sort of emotional debt. The offer "Here, take what you need, all I have is yours" is not so kind, if it comes with a secret demand in return. You get the idea.

It is said in many myths that Satan, more than being hideous and blunt, will readily appear as a shimmer of God—attractive if not clear, a seeming shortcut to all that is beautiful. Such are the near enemies of authenticity. They masquerade as qualities—even dreams of a self we aspire to become—that sometimes have little to do with who we really are. My friend, the

Reverend Charles Gibbs, is executive director of the United Religions Initiative, a grassroots global effort devoted to interfaith cooperation. Recently, we were walking near the San Francisco Bay when he said, "It doesn't take much courage to have grandiose dreams."

When I asked him to explain, he suggested that sometimes we are seduced to imagine an ambition so elevated that it keeps us from getting our hands dirty, that pining for it only keeps us from doing any real work in the world. The golden aspiration is so unreachable that it makes us feel good without having to really risk getting involved. Our grandiosity is conveniently insulated from critique or accountability because of its noble intent. In actuality, it might take more fortitude to face our pain and limitations and then do good anyway, in spite of all our failings.

In his autobiography, *Memories, Dreams, Reflections*, Carl Jung recounts his wrestling with a dream that freed him from his elevated self. He dreamt that he and a primitive man had tracked down a noble and learned professor by the name of Siegfried, who seemed virtuous and committed to the highest ideals. To his surprise, Jung and the primitive man then murdered Siegfried. This dream so troubled Jung that he wrote to a friend that he felt compelled to solve its meaning or he would have to take his own life. He felt an urgent need to face what was under this dream in order to go on. Eventually, he realized that Siegfried was his distanced noble self, his golden ego—the near enemy of altruism. And the dream was telling Jung that it was necessary to silence all his ambitions, no matter how noble, in order to free himself from the trappings of his ego.

Later, Jung concluded that he would never have been open enough to discover the Unconscious had he not put Siegfried to rest. The dream, it turned out, was instructing Jung to remove all the masks he had taken such care in carving for himself—even the beautiful ones. This is an important lesson for us all. Otherwise, any good work we might accomplish will only feed our secret needs. Indeed, Dante has a special ring in purgatory for those who do good poorly, which often comes from doing good unconsciously.

The truth is that being a humanitarian starts with helping a stranger clean up their broken jar of mayonnaise in the parking lot, though the slivers might cut you. And make no mistake, to stop the smallest bleeding, whether done gracefully or awkwardly, is a remarkable thing in itself.

So forget imagined greatness. Forget dreaming of being the one to cure cancer, unless that is your honest-to-God call. Otherwise, intoxicating our days with being "the one" is the near enemy of hope. When we dream of being a famous savior rather than ache to alleviate the inch of suffering that is before us, we are chasing our noble self. Rather than dreaming of scenes of applause, we need to somehow slay that hungry ghost and help each other accept our humble need to be loved. Then we can get to work.

Tendencies

If you don't know where you're going, turn around and
make sure you know where you're coming from.
❖ *African saying*

Earlier we talked about living within patterns. Here we will explore the tendencies we develop through experience, and focus
on the nature of our tendencies—our bag of familiar responses—
and how they become patterns.

Let's start with some stories. There are always stories. The first
goes like this. Once realizing he was on the path to Nirvana,
Buddha refused to leave his human form until he relived each of
his previous lives as a fully, compassionate being. This is an interesting response to the earned chance to leave suffering behind.
Why would an enlightened being choose to relive his former,
more limited selves? Not to redo or correct his life and certainly
not to go back. But, once we are awakened and conscious and
aware, the question remains: how do we come to peace with our
experience of being human over time?

The counterpoint to Buddha's want to make peace with his
humanness is the well-known story of Lot's wife, who, warned by
God not to look back, couldn't resist and so turned into a pillar
of salt. It seems when we are unconscious and unaware, the urge
to look back is seldom healing or integrating, but more often an
escape from facing what is necessary to stay authentic. Reliving

the past under these circumstances can drain us of what makes us human and turn us bitter. Of course, it's never very clear what our small glances back will do to us. To be sure, though, we each have the capacity to enter our Buddha nature or to turn to salt. So understanding our tendencies—both toward where we've been and where we're going—seems necessary if we are to engage the past and our patterns of living in a way that is liberating and not constricting.

This leads to a conversation about the Hindu notion of karma. Now the popular understanding of karma is rather like a westernized cartoon of a very profound aspect of the spiritual condition of being human. Often oversimplified, karma is rendered in broad strokes by westerners as living many lives under the threat that if you're bad in one life, you'll be punished in the next—or the reverse. But let's look more closely.

The word *karma* comes from the Sanskrit root *kri*, meaning *to do*; *kri*, in turn, is from the Pali, *kamma*, meaning *action, effect, destiny, the work of fate*. Weaving these notions into their largest meaning, the original Hindu sense of karma refers to the sum of all the consequences of a person's actions in this or a previous life. We must consider the phrase "previous life" in various ways: literally, as well as referring to different passages within a single life of transformation on earth. With this in mind, we are responsible for the impact of our actions over time. Once we've formed our tendencies to act, we have the option of following them or resisting them.

This freedom to follow our tendencies or not resides in the well of what the Hindus call *atman*, or *the breath of spirit and consciousness within*. Our surrender to God is believed to be essential in dissolving the bonds of destructive tendencies. And so

obeying the breath of spirit and consciousness within (our atman, or the God within) is believed to be instrumental in creating life-nourishing tendencies. Given that what is not integrated
is repeated, destructive tendencies, if not faced and dismantled,
repeat themselves, not only throughout one life but throughout
many lives. This is the psycho-spiritual dynamic at the heart of
karma. And no one is exempt from it.

So the challenge for each of us centers on understanding our
own eternal journey in terms of which of our personal tendencies are life nourishing and which are destructive, which are we
upholding and which are we resisting. Paradoxically, only being
human on earth can offer up the experience of spirit necessary
to alter our tendencies.

My first encounter with facing my own tendencies surfaced
abruptly when waiting for surgery to determine if I had brain
cancer. Four or five of us were all lined up in the anteroom of
the operating room, and one by one the masked angels of this
medical underworld were hooking us up. My fear kept building.
I thought I might explode. Next to me was a young woman, a
poor, innocent, inexperienced being. She was terrified of the
needle that would make her sleep. So terrified, she moaned
before the needle touched her skin. Her moan was piercing. I
reached for her but was tethered by my own IV. But this was her
karma. The needle wouldn't take, and they had to try four, five,
six times until it settled in a vein. I lay there on my back, my last
pouch of innocence torn. And I thought, "Who will suture this?"
I watched her moan and thought, "What on earth is my karma?
What do I fear and need to relinquish so deeply that I am here?"

I had always needed closure, had always planned the days minutely in advance, but as I struggled with cancer, it became clear—there would be no closure. It made me wonder if there ever is closure or is it just a fabrication like time, a rope of mind which humans need to braid and knot in order to get by. But there I was. The terrified young woman was wheeled off. And then they came for me. As I was rolled into the operating room, as I began to drift, I remember pressing the question: *is lack of closure my needle, which—because I fear it—must be thrust at me four, five, six times until it settles in my spirit's vein?*

Up to that point in my life, I had thought of hardships as inexplicable events happening to me and others and viewed strength as the ability to endure these unwanted circumstances. Such endurance is certainly a strength. But for the first time, laying there next to this terrified young woman, waiting my turn, my sense of all this changed. Suddenly I understood strength in another way, as the character revealed by facing what comes our way—until our tendencies and habits are revealed to us, until they wrestle or dance with us, until we are worn into who we are born to be.

A few years later, seemingly on the other side—though there has never been a going back—I was waiting for my third annual checkup when a vain and beautiful woman, close to forty, sat next to me. It was a golden afternoon, and everything about her was claiming herself a tragedy. We talked a bit, and she admitted as much, then gave me her arm, peppered with needle marks. I looked into her eyes and wondered, "Who am I to minimize her pain?" Yet it was clear that she wanted me to minimize her pain. It made me realize how the Universe improvises its balance. How a horse thief becomes a horse. How a blacksmith becomes an anvil. How my surgeon will become a gardener. How the wings of one life are broken to form a nest in which someone is born who can go everywhere while going nowhere.

I continue to envy such transformations. Ironically, I asked for so long to see with the freshness of the first man, and humbly I had to give up a rib in order to go on. It's clear the obstacles will shape us if we let them. Now, years on, I ache for someone to minimize my pain. At times, I'd like to run away but can't, for I must have done that once before.

Believing the Guest

Often, we promise
what can't be promised.

It is not a matter of lying.
Though sometimes we lie.
More that the hawk's wings
can't cover the sky.

Over the years, I've discovered that as I grow more accepting of my humanness, limitations and all, I am less blind to the humanness and limitations of others. I find I can accept others more fully and with fewer expectations. The more wholly I can see them, the more holy they become. The more integrated we become, the more we are able to behold the integrity of the life around us. I was astonished to experience this obvious yet profound truth.

I can also see now how I promoted inauthentic relationships when loving others in fragmented ways that refused the truth of their wholeness. For instance, I have a friend who for years would repeatedly surface at the most unexpected times with sly and cutting remarks. These lances hurt, and I was always surprised. Even after twenty years, I was always stunned to receive these jabs. It just didn't seem like her. She was so kind and thoughtful. I've come to understand that this, too, is part of who she is. My continual surprise was not the result of some noble sense of innocence on my part, but of my denial of this lapse in her character. This striking out is part of her wholeness, and I was refusing to accept all of who she has repeatedly shown herself to be, which she at some level wants me to see. The sudden appearance of all we are capable of, of all those we love are capable of, is the guest we seldom want to believe.

Another poignant example is of a dear friend who has fallen in love with a crack addict. He says that things are wonderful when she's not using, and then she unleashes a dark, cruel temperament that is unbearable. Later, she returns with sweetness and apologies and promises, and my friend is drawn back in, confiding to me, "She's so special and dear when not using. That's *the her* I love. The other isn't the real her."

In this way, he divides his knowledge of this woman, refusing to face the truth of all of her. As long as he fragments his sense of her, he doesn't have to accept or deal with the total truth of who she is. We do such strange things in the name of love.

His case is acutely clear, but we all find ourselves here from time to time. As long as we quarantine parts of our humanness from each other, we end up elevating the sides of ourselves and loved ones we wish to see and exiling those aspects we don't want to face. This only exacerbates our relationships, allowing us to deflect responsibility for our humanness and the effect of our limitations on those around us.

In my own life, I have felt this painfully in a way that has consumed a friendship of thirty years. This oldest of friends would from time to time erupt with anger and frustration. When we examined what was wrong, he claimed there was an inequity in our relationship, usually tracing back to me. We would face it and try to correct our course. In fairness, a good many things did trace back to me. I kept being diligent in trying to be a good friend. Since there was a lot I had to learn about friendship, it took many years for me to see what was mine and what was his. Eventually, his anger and accusation didn't go away, no matter what I did. In fact, it erupted into an envy and hostility that I could no longer dismiss as another bad day or as a reaction to some mistake I had made. The dark issues kept repeating even though we'd dealt with them several times.

I so wanted to isolate these outbursts as not really him. We were so close and had such history that I feared if I lost him, I'd lose myself. But his anger and woundedness at life had no bottom. He was a wolf of discontent who would ignore his hunger till he had to ravage whatever was near. And in my need to be loved, I was always near. Finally, his striking out was so painful that I was forced to accept that, as long as he would not face his bottomless wound, it was not safe to be around him. Because we both had refused the truth of our wholeness for so long, our friendship, sweet in so many other ways, was in jeopardy.

This difficult passage has cost us our friendship. This is not to say that he is bad. He is not. Just troubled. And unable to climb out of his trouble. This is not to say that I don't still love him. Ironically, I love him more honestly but can't subject myself to his hurtfulness anymore because I love myself more honestly now as well. I still miss him.

So what does all this say about the art of facing things and healthy love? Mostly that we can take better care of ourselves. So often we want love so badly that we allow ourselves to be violated, afraid that if we acknowledge the obvious we will lose the love we have. What we don't face in ourselves is that such violations *are not loving*. The loss is already underway.

When we are slapped, verbally or physically, we stall the work of love when we say, "They didn't mean it," rather than face the troublesome fact that, even loving you, they did mean it. And when we are the ones doing the slapping, we stall our own inner growth when we exonerate ourselves by claiming we didn't mean it. Instead, the challenge is to try to understand the humbling fact that we are not as noble as we think we are. Being human, everyone is capable of such violations. But the work of love is facing our capacity to hurt each other however it appears. The love is in how we care enough to own and correct ourselves. In fact, the noblest work we can do is to understand and accept our humanness in all its limited ways and *still* devote ourselves to loving each other.

There Is Something Else There

I will bear my loneliness
like a planet that cannot
deny its orbit around
the pull of what is true.

When we speak of wholeheartedness, we are not talking about sorting our experience and feelings like mail, but more about the necessary art of receiving and integrating all that comes our way and how that expands, deepens, and strengthens our world and life view. What makes Abraham Lincoln such a remarkable example of wholeheartedness was his depth and resilience to stand by his core during storms of personal and national duress that we can only imagine. He seemed to be an intensely authentic individual who suffered greatly and deeply all that he experienced. He himself described his bouts with melancholy. He was an introvert painfully called into public service at a critical time in our nation's history. Historians have described Lincoln as married to doubt. Today, he would most likely have been diagnosed with depression.

Somehow, he neither steeled himself to what he felt, nor did he become paralyzed in the sadness and trouble he carried. During his presidency, he and Mary Todd Lincoln lost their son, Willie, to an inexplicable ailment that may have come from the Washington Canal, a public dump where the National Mall is now, in which garbage and dead horses were thrown. Willie's death was a terrible loss. At the same time, Lincoln bore the weight of the Civil War ripping the country apart. He carried constantly the prospect that losing this war would allow freedom to perish. It would mean that the American experiment of democracy would fail.

It was during the summer months that he and his family moved three miles north of the Capitol to the Soldier's Home. Here, disabled veterans from the War of 1812 hobbled around the grounds, playing checkers and feeling for limbs no longer there. From his porch, he could look past them and see the Capitol, half-built in his day, a symbolic reminder of how fragile and in progress America truly was. In all, Lincoln spent one quarter of his presidency living on the grounds of the Soldier's Home. It was in this cottage that he drafted the Emancipation Proclamation.

Mary Todd wanted them to move to the cottage to get away from the overwhelming pressures of Washington, so they might have proper space to mourn their son. But the sanctuary proved a much-needed crucible in which the unprecedented tragedies of his family and his country weighed on him terribly. At nights, unable to sleep, he'd walk the nearby cemetery, which would later become Arlington National Cemetery. In the mornings, upon first rising, he could see the contraband camps, where homeless, emancipated slaves of the District of Columbia lived if they had nowhere to go. He went to sleep and woke to the huddled brokenness of his people: free but poor, spit out from war, soldiers buried around him, and his own dead son, whose face seemed just out of reach. Is it any wonder that on his daily horse ride to the White House, he seemed burdened and distracted into some otherworldly place? As if God were leading him into a darkness he couldn't run from but only live through.

Along the way, on Vermont Avenue, a full-bearded poet in his forties would rock on his porch and nod to the president. It was Walt Whitman. He had been living in Washington several months, visiting the wounded and working part-time at the Union Army paymaster's office. On August 12, 1863, he wrote of seeing Lincoln:

I see the President almost every day. I saw him this morning about 8:30 coming in to business, riding . . . near L street. He always has the company of twenty-five or thirty cavalry, with sabers drawn . . . They say this guard was against his personal wish . . . Mr. Lincoln on the saddle generally rides a good-sized, easy-going gray horse, is dress'd in plain black, somewhat rusty and dusty, wears a black stiff hat, and looks about as ordinary . . . as the commonest man . . . I see very plainly Abraham Lincoln's dark brown face, with the deep-cut lines, the eyes, always . . . with a deep latent sadness . . . We have got so that we exchange bows, and very cordial ones . . . Sometimes one of his sons, a boy of ten or twelve, accompanies him, riding at his right on a pony . . . They pass'd me once very close, and I saw the President in the face fully, as they were moving slowly, and his look, though abstracted, happen'd to be directed steadily in my eye. He bow'd and smiled, but far beneath his smile I noticed well the expression I have alluded to . . . There is something else there.

Lincoln had the capacity to somehow keep his heart open until his mind could find clarity at the other end of all he felt. With everyone demanding him to act in different ways—with some demanding emancipation sooner than he felt possible and others demanding retribution on the South—he succumbed to neither. Somehow, he endured his full humanity until it enabled a vision of the whole, of history and eternity. Lincoln demonstrated a hard but beautiful truth: that receiving our full humanity—not denying it or blocking it—is the climb that brings us to a view of the ages. For being fully human opens up the eternal. Through the strength of that vulnerability, he had the resolve to apply that vision with compassion in all directions. This was an example of spiritual leadership we have rarely seen.

It took tremendous courage. It is a challenge we all face in our own ways, in our own days: to *not* act prematurely and to *not* act in pressured response to the momentums that surround us, but to retain our ability to act in concert with that depth we call truth. Imagine that we're swimmers who must hold our breath in order to get below the surface currents pushing us about. And yet, once that far down, we must still have the strength to bring what we know of the deep back through those currents to the surface. At times, we each must retreat from the push and pull of the world in order to know our own minds and hearts deeply. Then we must have the courage not to stay there, but to bring what we know of the deep back into our lives and the world. In this capacity, Lincoln was our modern Job.

Speaking to Lincoln's depth of mood and clarity of action, John Hay, a senior White House aide, remarked that the president had an "elasticity of spirit." This apt phrase describes the resiliency needed to go deeply within and to return to the currents of life around us. It is this resiliency that we all need in order to sustain the necessary journey between our inner search for meaning and our outer obligations to care for the world we inherit.

Often, people give up the journey back and forth because it is so hard. The visionary poet William Blake gave up the trek back into the world, hiking further and further into his interior climbs. It is why his Prophetic Books are so indecipherable. Others, like Charles Darwin and Thomas Edison, have chosen to stay squarely in the world. These two pioneers worked like great mechanics at the machinery of nature. But the paradoxical task is to keep the two—the inner world of meaning and the outer world of care—in balance and connected.

Lincoln kept the two connected, and the emotional cost was great. He felt largely alone. It impacted his sense of leadership. It is well known that Lincoln couldn't find the right general for the Union troops, though he finally settled for Ulysses S. Grant. He was heard to remark one night at the cottage in frustration, "It is the soil of *one* nation. None of them ever gets this." His capacity to suffer let him never forget that Southerners suffered, too. To exile the vanquished Southerners was merely to secede in aftermath.

It's piercing and jarring to realize that Lincoln was assassinated on Good Friday, April 14, 1865, just a few days after Robert E. Lee surrendered at Appomattox. In an inexplicable braid of the mysterious and the tragic, which he himself foretold in his second inaugural, his blood seemed to be drawn so that the nation could resurrect: "Yet, if God wills that it continue . . . until every drop of blood drawn with the lash, shall be paid by another drawn with the sword . . . it must be said 'the judgments of the Lord are true and righteous.'"

I was in Washington, D.C. last week. It was beautiful. The cherry blossoms had come and gone, blooming only for five to nine days in early April. The dried petals on the ground were poignant. That night I went to the Lincoln Memorial and stared long into the stone face that took Daniel Chester French so many years to carve. I don't know if it was me or the day or the residue of that gentle giant reluctantly serving as the Atlas of a torn America, but I could see, like Whitman, the weight of all he carried. The stone eyes cast the clearness of a still lake just before a storm. Then, backing out into the open, I stood on the very square from which Martin Luther King, Jr. gave his remarkable speech. I turned, and in the reflecting pool I saw, only for an instant, the messy tangle of humanity trying to sort itself. I thought all inaugurals should take place here.

For we all are called to keep beginning. And sooner or later, like Lincoln, we are all led into a darkness we can't run from but only live through. The story of his vulnerable strength and "elasticity of spirit" serves as a compelling example of how wholeheartedness can help us through the twists and pulls of real living.

Such wholeheartedness is not abstract, but a muscular, elastic way of engaging life with demanding skills. Lincoln models three of those skills: to somehow endure our full humanity until it scours a clear seeing that enables a vision of the whole that brings us to a view of the ages; to find the courage to *not* act prematurely and to *not* act in pressured response to the momentums that surround us, but to retain our ability to act in concert with that view of the ages we call truth; and to stay committed to the journey back and forth between what is inner and what is outer, to keep the inner world of meaning and the outer world of care connected.

As Whitman said, there is something else there. In each of us.

Wholeheartedness

I don't understand.
But God is the unseen thing
that connects my heart to the stars.

Wholeheartedness is perhaps the most significant resource we have and, as such, one of the hardest to talk about. We can only point to it briefly. Like Jacob and the nameless angel at the bottom of the ravine, we are left to wrestle with it in the middle of the night, not letting go until it blesses us. For with it, we are connected to everything. When holding nothing back, it can bestow eyes within our eyes and ears within our ears. Without it, we often feel insignificant, and that insignificance has its own contagion until we think whatever we might manage here on earth is of no consequence in the face of the enormity of time.

From under that cloud, it is a short stumble into the oppressive feeling that life itself is insignificant. Though our connection to the Whole seems elusive and intangible, there is much at stake—namely, whether we live or watch. Here, we come face to face with a deeper sense of courage needed to be truly alive. As the poet Jack Gilbert says, "Courage is not abnormal . . . not the marvelous act, but the evident conclusion of being."

And our chief means toward that sublime conclusion of being is the courage to use all of our heart. Anything less and we risk a gray existence. The poet Jane Hirshfield puts it this way:

To live fully and willingly in the world of the living is more brave even than going open-eyed toward death. All too often we do neither, and, clinging to some safer middle ground, end by feeling neither our terrors nor our joys.

In the larger culture, we have been steered away from whole-heartedness by gross misperceptions. This is made stunningly clear in a small compelling book called *Prayers of the Cosmos*. It returns the words of Jesus to the original language he spoke, Aramaic, the native Middle Eastern tongue of his day. In it, we discover, after all these years, that what we have translated as "be you perfect" (*nethqadash*) really means "be you all-embracing." What we have translated as "Heaven" (*d'bwashmaya*) means "Universe," and what we have translated as "lead us not into temptation" (*wela tablan l'nesyuna*) is closer to "Do not let surface things delude us . . . free us from what holds us back."

These mistranslations appear in other traditions as well. *Tamim* was an Old Testament Hebrew word meaning *wholehearted*. But it was translated in the King James Version of the Bible as *perfect*. These confining missteps narrow the path of what it means to be alive, resulting in a limited frame of mind that still plagues us in the modern age. For when we aim to be *wholehearted* and *all-embracing*, we live one life. When we aim to be *perfect* and *unblemished*, we live quite another.

These are profound differences upon which thousands of years of moral guidance have been based. It seems we've taken a wrong turn! Accepting this and correcting this are rife with difficulties. It's like telling those of us in the ninth generation that the home our ancestors bequeathed, the one we now preserve as sacred, was built on a sinkhole. Urgent as such news is, we cannot ignore that the discovery of such a misperception can be ripping. To *be* wholehearted, the uncovering of thousands of years of moral misguidance must be approached with compassion. Otherwise, we undo ourselves. So how might we repair these spiritual missteps? It's too much for any one person, yet one soul at a time leaning into the courage to be all-embracing is more powerful than it seems.

If we trace how the major traditions of the Middle East unfolded before these mistranslations, we find that Judaism, Christianity, and Islam stem from the same source, and probably the same language. All originally called God either *El* or *Al*, which means *The One* or *That One which expresses itself uniquely through all beings*. From this arose the sacred names *Elohim* (Hebrew) and *Allah* (Arabic).

Imagine, we are all expressions of the same Original Being, and much of our lives are spent recovering that deep knowing. This notion of God as a Divine Presence that keeps expressing itself uniquely through all beings and our journey to rediscover that we share the same truth is at the heart of the Hindu concept *Tat Tvam Asi*, which is Sanskrit for *Thou Art That*. We referred to this earlier. The scholar Eugene Kennedy describes Thou Art That as "the most significant teaching [of] compassion; which requires that we die to our smaller selves in order to rise to [a] vision that reveals that we share the same human nature with all other persons."

Hard as it is at times to accept, we are each other: as beautiful as the next and as brutal. And rightly, what's brutal in each other engenders fear. If unaddressed, such fear can force us to live by how different we are. In contrast, being wholehearted can lead to the discovery of our shared human nature. In essence, realizing we are each other—*Thou Art That*—helps alleviate fear. As the Isa Upanishad reveals:

Who sees all beings in his own Self
and his own Self in all beings,
loses all fear.

So here we are, two thousand years later, dusting off the misconceptions to find that we are asked, and have always been asked, to be wholehearted more than perfect. To free ourselves from all that holds us back. To enter life with our hearts wide open. To embrace both our terrors and our joys. And to honor that we are all made of the same filaments of being. For this is our best chance at quieting fear—our best chance at hearing the almost inaudible sigh of God opening His eyes by opening ours.

Beginner's Heart

I need to take a sacred pause,
as if I were a sun-warmed rock
in the center of a rushing river.

❖ *Dawna Markova*

Archbishop Desmond Tutu speaks of how the omnipotent God we worship chooses to be impotent in the world, unless God's work is manifest through the collaboration of human beings. In this, God entrusts the world to us. And so the miracle rests with us and is seldom spectacular, but more the work of humble people choosing to give what they have. By doing so, we become vehicles of the Divine, not in being a spokesperson for the mind of God—no one can claim that—but more, in being a conduit of the vitality that keeps everything alive. "In this way," the archbishop says, "You may have the chance to wipe tears from the eyes of someone who will then know that they matter, that they are loved." This, he says, is Godly work.

This brings to mind the story of Jeremy who was a likable but odd boy, somewhat of a loner. His parents found it difficult to teach him responsibility. He was forever losing things. He'd come home, having misplaced a new sweater or a knapsack. His parents tried to discipline him so he would value things, but nothing seemed to work. Once, he came home having lost his sneakers. He just walked in barefoot and went to his room. When scolded, he shrugged, said he was sorry and that he'd try harder to keep track of his belongings.

Tragically, Jeremy died in an auto accident in his junior year. It was devastating. When his parents attended the school memorial, they were stunned to see hundreds of students show up. One after another spoke of how kind and generous Jeremy was, of how he was always helping others. One boy told how his single mother couldn't afford to buy him shoes and how Jeremy pulled him aside, unlaced his sneakers, and gave them to him. A girl told how she didn't have a jacket in winter and how Jeremy, seeing her shiver, gave her his sweater. On and on, students stepped forward to pay tribute to this young, quiet conductor of kindness who gave everything away. His parents were undone, and the students softened to learn of each other. Jeremy, at such a young age, was an anonymous seed. In some strange way, everyone who had been given something by Jeremy now shared a special friendship. They looked around at each other, like distant relatives, with a quiet eagerness to know each other better.

I thought about changing his name in telling his story, but something caught in my throat at the thought of it. For his name and the name of those like him should be sung into the night. Jeremy, who, for some reason, didn't hesitate to give anything away. Jeremy, who kept his sacred calling to himself. Jeremy, who, like the sages and saints of the past, taught us that giving creates a bond that makes relatives of strangers. Jeremy, who would vanish into the humble satisfaction of pure giving, like a wave that has done its work softening the shore. Jeremy, Jeremy, Jeremy.

One lesson here is that if you want to discover the bond that exists between all human beings, give freely to anyone you find in need. For giving freely invokes gratitude. And giving and gratitude, like the two poles of electricity, spark the current of intimacy, known as life force, which connects everything. We could call the place where true giving (generosity) and true receiving (gratitude) lead us—Beginner's Heart. Where Beginner's Mind allows us to glimpse the totality of life freshly, Beginner's Heart allows us to experience that totality, the rush of which has made hardened soldiers cry. Of course, at their deepest, Beginner's Mind and Beginner's Heart are one and the same—just different paths to the same center. And stories such as Jeremy's affirm that generosity and gratitude are never very far from us, that we are born with them and carry them under our skin.

If we want to collaborate with God, as Archbishop Tutu suggests, we simply have to give what we have, like Jeremy and the boy in the Hindu teaching story who wanted a drum. They both accepted what they were given and passed it on to those in need. Whether it was a loaf of bread, a pot, a sweater, or a pair of sneakers, they accepted their place as a carrier of gifts. It seems we do Godly work when we let things pass through us with love. This is one way we know we have returned to a Beginner's Heart, when we feel the things of life move through us, with our blessing, to others.

Trust of This Kind

To be invested with dignity means to represent something
more than oneself.
❖ Abraham Heschel

The Akasha Field

In the summer of 2004, I was in Barcelona attending the World
Parliament of Religions. One morning, I was sitting with a
crowd listening to Dr. Ervin Laszlo, a scientist and philosopher
trained at the Sorbonne in Paris. He was speaking through trans-
lators about the *Akasha Field*.

In Sanskrit, the word *Akasha* refers to a collective presence
and memory among human beings. In the West we tend to ignore this idea, insisting we are separate and unattached. Yet there
is molecular and biological evidence of our Oneness and how
our very presence influences each other, how being influences
being. These are not arguments to persuade, but glimpses of the
fabric of life from which to draw vitality and strength. It is becoming more and more evident that we have an innate call to
find each other and join. To begin with, it is now well-established
that when placing two living heart cells from different people in
a petri dish, they will over time find a third common beat.

Dr. Laszlo went on to describe similar experiments with atoms. Once atoms A and B have been vibrating in harmony, atom

A is placed in close proximity to a third unrelated atom, P. Amazingly, the vibration and harmony generated and experienced by atoms A and B is imparted to atom P. The reverse appears to be true as well. When atom A is left with the unrelated atom P until they vibrate in harmony, and then atom A is returned to its more familiar partner, atom B, the vibration and harmony generated and experienced by atoms A and P is then imparted to the more familiar atom B.

The same situation has been explored with meditators, and the same results have appeared. When Archie and Betty, who are intimates (partners, family, or friends), meditate together, their brain waves quickly harmonize. At this point, Archie is asked to meditate with a complete stranger, Petra, and, amazingly, the state of harmonized brain waves is quickly imparted to the stranger, Petra. *This suggests that the condition of intimacy is a catalyst for the experience of Oneness.* All of this infers that there is a cosmic, unified field of presence, very near to us all, that ranges from atoms to cells to souls. The crucial question, then, is: how do we relate to this field? How do we tap into its energy and resources?

As I was watching Dr. Laszlo speak, his words were swiftly being translated in clear booths into four languages at once, being whispered into everyone's ears. I realized that what he was suggesting was happening there in Barcelona. I was part of a short-term community of over eight thousand people from all over the world who had come together because of a common belief in something larger than our selves. Regardless of our many faces and names, there was something shimmering there between us, like the vibration and harmony generated by those atoms put in close proximity with each other.

It made me wonder, hasn't this always been the power of communities of care that somehow break through the trance of their times? Isn't this descriptive of the throngs surrounding Buddha under the Bodhi tree? Or the hundreds gathered to hear Jesus at the Sermon on the Mount? Or the thousands following Gandhi's march of salt to the Indian Ocean? Or the million crowding the mall in Washington to hear Martin Luther King, Jr. give his landmark speech? Isn't this the mystery of self-organizing moments of collective presence?

These instances confirm that there is a subtle, if mysterious, presence that cradles us all, if we can access the Akasha Field and enliven it. Actually, it doesn't take much, once we are opened, to feel the pull of things coming together—whether that be atoms vibrating, strangers meditating, or hundreds gathering around an elder's presence. Like someone watching a river from its bank, the current seems impossibly fast until we step down and enter. But in the center of the current, the ever-present flow of life is illuminating and vital. In the center of the current, we are swept along into the very nature of how things grow.

How Many Ways to Grow an Arm

An expert in cell biology, Dr. Bruce Carlson, director of the Institute of Gerontology at the University of Michigan, has pioneered research in limb development and regeneration. In conversation, he conveyed a startling fact about the fundamental nature of how life grows. He began to describe morphogenetic fields, a phenomenon that has remained a mystery to scientists since the beginning of the 1900s. In such a field, a group of cells, like those assembling to begin their embryonic growth into a human arm, demonstrate a remarkable property of regeneration. If this cluster of cells is split in half, like a worm cut in half, each will grow into an arm. If two clusters of such cells are joined, they will merge and grow into one arm. If such a cluster is cut up into smaller pieces, they will reorganize, find each other, and grow into one arm.

The fact of this is remarkable. Dr. Carlson suggests that this is a fundamental, biological condition. More than an analogy, this is a biospiritual property of the very nature of existence that holds Wholeness as an inevitable state and love as a force equal to gravity that, if allowed, will move living things toward that state of Wholeness. This inevitable impetus toward Wholeness informs our many senses of human community as more than a dream, but as part of life's regeneration system. Whether it be family, friendships, tribes, clans, or the complex hives of culture, we are all brought into life with an innate impulse to become whole if we are split, to merge into one when we are joined, and, most importantly, to reorganize and heal when we are broken into smaller pieces.

This provides a cellular context for the Christian notion that where two or more are gathered, the Holy Spirit is present, and for the Buddhist notion of sanghas as communities of mindful beings invoking awakened lives more effectively together than alone. It provides a biological basis for how wounded lives gathering in twelve-step rooms or in cancer groups are stronger in each other's presence than when struggling in isolation. It proves why relationship-centered care—that is, the notion that relationships are part of the medicine—works.

The mysterious truth of morphogenetic fields implies that it is the social constructs—the complications of our human will—

that impede these innate, regenerative forces. It is often the social dis-eases of our will that prevent us from joining, merging, and healing into new wholes.

The Four Trusts

Trust of this kind—in the common presence of all things; in the fact that no matter how we are split, we will regenerate and heal; in the blessing that true intimacy will open us to Oneness; and trust that what churns up our bottom only deepens our flow— these mark *the fullness of trust in God*, which Sufis call *Tawakkul.*

I ask you, how do these four trusts appear in your life? Which are your strengths? Which need more attention? What is your history with the four trusts? When have you been aware of the presence of all things, and what has that felt like? In what ways have you witnessed or experienced the mysterious process of regeneration? Tell the story of a "split that has grown back." How has true intimacy deepened your experience of life itself? By intimacy, I mean more than sex, but that safe truth-telling space that unfolds between two human beings when the humility of being alive opens the heart's eye. And tell the story of a time when life churned up your bottom, and how that hurt, and how, when the disturbance settled, you were deeper for it. If you haven't experienced these forms of trust, search for them and talk about them. For the questions and the stories call them to our side the way native chants invite corn to grow.

In truth, our relationship and comfort with these things never stand still. For me, the doorway to my work as a poet was shut until I could accept the common presence of all things. And cancer taught me to surrender to however life wanted to churn up my bottom. And the quiet days on the other side taught me that, when too exhausted to try anymore, I still was able to re-generate and heal. I am here to say that, after much painful churning, my masks have dissolved, and all of it has deepened my flow. And in the days that remain, I keep learning how true inti-macy, the art of facing the full humanity of one another, is a blessing that surprises me into the vast meadow of Oneness where the unblocked light brings everything full term.

I only know that risking these fundamental trusts enables us to experiment with the humble will to love, which, in turn, gives us access to the very fabric of life. I only know that, with-out such trust, we can turn blunt and cruel. At the heart of it, that we will fail and fall and make mistakes is not newsworthy. It is in facing what we've done or failed to do and how we get up that our character is defined. It is in what we choose to lean on when getting up that we leave our suffered marks on the earth. I only know that when face down, I have heard the breath of the Universe whisper, *"If you could settle into the silence beneath your fear, you'd come to the shore between life and death and simply hold each other."*

Building on the Past

The past is a road of initiation, not victimization.
✧ *Angeles Arrien*

Ruin is an odd term for what's left after time distills all our intent. It implies that in our haste to find the future we have missed the point of those who came before. The word *artifact* refers to *something made by human craft*. At least here we hold what others made with some degree of wonder. But every part of history has immense meaning in its own moment. This is where wisdom hides, if we can empathize enough to open another's time. When we can uncover the meaning carried in things, we begin to build on the past. In this regard, we are talking about finding fragments of what matters, which, put together, begin to tell us how to live. It's interesting that the word *relic* means *that which remains, something worthy of reverence*. Routinely, it is only our distance from things that determines whether we think we are holding a ruin, an artifact, or a relic. On the contrary, it seems our task, whether sifting through old civilizations or old relationships, is to draw close enough to what has been till we can behold the worthy part of what remains. This is the meaning of legacy: the courage to care for what has brought us this far, the courage to decipher the truth in that which remains.

Too often, in our hunger to build our way out of a problem, we kill a great many things to make a road, when a simple path would do. Too often, our want to leave the noise and enter the jungle is self-defeating when we cut down the jungle to pave the way. James Thurber once sat by his window watching a bulldozer clear a field of elm trees for the building of an asylum intended for those driven insane by the taking down of elm trees. We tend to do this.

Still, no one can solve the past. We rightfully fear the oppression of thoughtless tradition. Yet wisdom is the liberating practice of applying the best of the past to living now. But whether considering the impact of yesterday or of Cain and Abel, it's hard to know what to do with what has come before. And everyone has advice.

Those living on water will say that when rowing, our back is toward the future as we stroke away from the past. And experienced rowers will tell you, "Pick a point on land behind you and keep the middle of your boat in line with it, and you will row steadily forward." And those living in the desert will say, "When climbing a mountain of sand, it is helpful to step in the footprints of others. The ghost of their weight will support your steps."

Here are three footprints. I leave the carving of oars to you.

What Was I to Do?

I became a historian, and went into the past, for the purpose of trying to understand and do something about what is going on in the present.

❖ *Howard Zinn*

I chanced to sit next to a country manager for the World Bank. He was responsible for helping to modernize Cambodia. It was a long flight, and we made our way beneath the pleasantries. I could tell that he carried a great weight. After a time, he told me the one story that plagues him.

"What was I to do?" he said, "These are impossible choices. We are committed to reducing poverty around the world. And sometimes this means hurting the few to help the many." He paused and rubbed his eyes, "It was determined that if we widened the stream to a canal in this old agricultural delta, it would triple the irrigation to their rice fields and this would triple the income of thousands of poor Cambodians—people who live on two hundred dollars a year. This simple widening of a stream would make it possible to construct low-income housing for thousands of the poor. But to build the canal, we had to tear down the oldest part of a village. We have to make these decisions all the time."

He loosened his tie. "We were told it takes character to withstand the pain of a few, if it will save so many. So, why do I feel dirty?" He tried to read my reactions. "You're imagining it already. I can tell by your eyes. Of course, there was this one old man living in a modest home that had been in his family for generations. His great grandfather was born in this house. He was born in this house. I paid him a fair subsidy. But still, the old man came to me, pleading, 'Please. Leave me in my home. Build around me. I'll live with the others. Don't destroy my ancestors! Please! I've never lived anywhere else!'"

The burdened manager rubbed his chest as if trying to remove a stain no one else could see. "I had no choice. We couldn't make an exception. They all would have wanted to stay." He took a swig from his small thimble of airplane gin. "Well, the day came and the old man wouldn't leave. I offered to help him, to take the smaller things that mattered to him, but he was inconsolable. I watched him weep in the rice field as the crane knocked down his home. I offered to drive him to a hotel where he could stay till his new home was built. I offered him more money, out of my own pocket. He wouldn't look at me or talk to me. He shuffled into the rice fields, shouted something in his native tongue and disappeared. I never saw him again." We both stared at the space between our seats. His voice went low. "Why can't I get him out of my mind?"

Near the River

We have to be present,
because our footprint on the world is so large.
❖ Betty Sue Flowers

In downtown Albany last spring, a parking lot adjacent to an office building was being torn apart to build another office building. There were bulldozers and surveyors and very busy men with hard hats reading blueprints in the wind, all pushing to meet someone else's deadline. But one day early on, while breaking ground, they stumbled onto broken bits of streets cobbled together. Construction was stopped, and teams of archeologists were brought in to try to understand what they were building on.

Instead of clearing for the future, everyone was suddenly uncovering the past. Unexpectedly, they had disturbed the remnants of a Dutch settlement that no one knew had been there. For six months, it captured the imagination of our small city. People would walk at lunchtime to see the silhouette of a three-hundred-year-old village beneath the grid of the archeologists' twine. You could see the partial walls of dwellings and even bits of what must have been rooms. The village was a seaport; the Hudson River had been much wider then.

They created a small exhibit of artifacts for everyone to see. And staring through the glass, I was taken by a partial ledger or book. The pages were half-shredded, and the script was faded and illegible. I kept staring at it. What were they trying to keep track of or say? Will this book in your hands now or the one you pick up next be buried and found like this? Will some fragment of today be deciphered tomorrow as something we had no understanding of?

By autumn, all the remnants were tagged and catalogued, and the site was closed up. Finally, a fresh foundation was built over the old, and the new construction was completed. When it opened, I entered the lobby of the new building and could feel the buried streets underneath. I closed my eyes and could imagine the noise of boxes falling in the cobbled street, causing the scribe to close his ledger and reenter the world. I stood there and realized that this new building will always be different than the others. Because in building it, we were compelled to unearth the old, compelled to understand who came before us a bit more. Now this spot holds a different place in the unspoken conscience of our community.

It's been a year, and what stays with me is this question of how to build on the past. For aren't we all pressed with excitement and necessity to build new homes, new relationships, new careers, new lives—always pressed by some real or imagined deadline, eager to get the thing done? Yet suddenly, if blessed, we trip on something of the past and, just as it feels that we are stalled, the thought appears that the need to dig in order to build might be God's way to unearth our foundation.

Belief in the Invisible

It was a small moment during Passover when I was a boy. We'd drive to Baldwin where my mother's parents lived. Pop was a furrier from Rumania. He had a great laugh which opened his entire face, and I was always drawn to peer through to a mysterious plateau where life had led him. He'd had his hardships: fleeing persecution in Europe as a boy, leaving his family, losing his brothers, crossing the cold Atlantic. And yet he'd landed through endless gratitude somewhere on God's invisible mountain where the air alone made him laugh.

Well, we'd drive the twenty minutes down Sunrise Highway to see them on Passover. And though we'd read the Haggadah and mouth the ancient blessings, recounting how God passed over the first born in another time, another place, it was the glass of wine left in the middle of the table for Elijah that taught me about faith. As done for centuries, the front door was left ajar, the filled glass set on the table as a quiet offering to the prophet-angel. And leaving the door open all night strangely made the world seem safer, bigger.

It made me realize at an early age that there is more power in inviting things in than in keeping things out. And leaving something out for an invisible guest has become a lifelong practice by which I bow to the mysteries, hoping they will show themselves. Like leaving bread for ducks to appear so we might see them take off in their splendor, much more colorful with their wings unfurled. Half of what I write is because I've left the door open for the invisible. The other half comes from living in the world. You see, Pop taught me that, no matter how little you have on your table, it's just as important to leave something for the invisible stranger as it is to save or give.

So Pop would play with us after dinner, chasing us from room to room. And suddenly, miraculously, he'd stop as we'd circle the cleaned up table, and with astonishment, he'd point to the half-empty glass and gasp, "Look! Elijah Was Here!" We were always dumbfounded. We'd get real close to the glass, to be sure the wine had actually been drunk. Then we'd race to the open door and look up and down the night-lit street. Once, I ran down the stoop, to the end of the block, and I swear I could almost feel the whip of Elijah's robe.

In a few years, my mother, thinking she was doing us a favor, let us know that Pop would somehow slip away and drink the wine. She said this not in malice, but as if she were arming us against a cruel world. But even knowing this did not undermine my belief in the unseen. For more than all of it—more than Pop's loving effort to have us believe and my mother's loving effort to have us see through it—more than this, I'm grateful to Pop for teaching me to always leave the door open. That while there are things to be afraid of, there is more to be thankful for.

Tensions of Awakening

To live a spiritual life we must first find the courage to enter into the desert of our loneliness and to change it by gentle and persistent efforts into a garden of solitude. This requires not only courage, but also a strong faith.

⋄ *Henri Nouwen*

When tired, I have to rest. When rested, I have to wake. When talking, I cannot hear. When listening, I cannot speak. And just as we must cycle daily between wakefulness and sleep, we are spiritually tied to rhythms that wake us as well as rhythms that numb us. In the course of our days, we are constantly negotiating qualities of being that enlarge or shrink our sense of life. There are too many such qualities to name, but some dynamic opposites stand out, from which we are asked to choose repeatedly.

To Broaden and Deepen or Narrow and Lessen

In *The Wisdom of the Crows*, a tale from the Jataka (birth stories of the Buddha), the Buddha-to-be is featured as a crow who gives instruction to a king. In stories of his previous lives, like this one, the Buddha is referred to as the *Bodhisatta*, which means *one on the path to awakening*. This differs from the term *Bodhisattva*, which means *one who has awakened, but who has chosen to stay in*

earthly relationship with others in support of a mutual enlightenment.
The stories from the Jataka imply that true awakening requires
many births and transformations. They offer a sense of how life
instructs us when our humanness traps us in a corner. In *The
Wisdom of the Crows*, the king has carelessly taken the advice of a
vengeful high priest to kill all the crows. In response:

*The Bodhisatta flew up into a Sal tree and sat there quietly, summoning
to his mind the ten perfections [those qualities that lead to awakening],
reviewing each one in turn:* Dana-parami—*generosity;* Sila-parami—
virtue; Nekkhama-parami—*renunciation;* Khanti-parami—*patience;*
Viriya-parami—*energy;* Aditthana-parami—*resolve; Metta-parami—
loving-kindness;* Sacca-parami—*truthfulness,* Pañña-parami—*wisdom;
and* Upekkha-parami—*equanimity.*

The Buddha-to-be considers each of these qualities and how
they might serve him in this situation, and then selects loving-
kindness (*Metta-parami*) as his guide. He then flies straight to
the palace and instructs the king in truthfulness (*Sacca-parami*)
and patience (*Khanti-parami*). The king's encounter with his own
Buddha nature—awakened in him by the Buddha-to-be as a
crow—causes him to broaden and deepen rather than to narrow
and lessen.

Here, as in so many wisdom traditions, we are offered ways to
enlarge our sense of things that will counter the ways that unfiltered experience can shrink our hearts. The question remains, if
Bodhisatta means *one on the path to awakening,* then what shall we
call *one on the path to numbness*? And if wholeheartedness is the

compass that keeps us on the path to awakening, then what are the many forms of partial heartedness that mislead us?

The truth is that we are always on the path to both, close to awakening and close to going numb. At each step, we are a breath and a choice away from being wholehearted or partial hearted. With each risk, we are a courage away from broadening and deepening or a hesitation from narrowing and lessening. Even given a devotion to sustained good choices, we are often asked to experience our limitations and failings as a way to grow, and so are further asked to restore wholeness when suffering partiality.

We've spoken of both sides throughout this book. Earlier, we spoke of the little decisions we all encounter—whether to hide instead of face, to lie instead of cry, to harden instead of staying vulnerable—and how our choices can lead to a narrowing, numb place from which we can bluntly hurt others. Letting the world in or keeping it out often depends on whether we enable distrust or trust, whether we affirm indirectness or directness, and whether we empower anonymous judgment or the courage to stand in one's truth without judging others. The lesser side of these choices can grow into small indulgences of the ego, so possible in anyone. These indulgences, if unchecked, can enable any of us to become demanding and even evil. Earlier, I referred to the film director Menno Meyjes, who traces Hitler's evil to a progression of heartless, smaller choices that remain very close to us all. Meyjes speaks of Hitler's "emotional cowardice, his relentless self-pity, his envy, his frustration, [and] the way he collects and nurtures offenses" and how these narrowing choices fueled an insatiable self-centeredness that turned uncontrollably destructive.

We also looked at the habits of thinking that the great Roman orator Cicero offered, which keep us a prisoner of ever-shrinking patterns. They are worth restating:

The illusion that personal gain is made up of crushing others;
The tendency to worry about things that cannot be changed
 or corrected;
Insisting that a thing is impossible because we cannot accomplish it;
Refusing to set aside trivial preferences;
Neglecting development and refinement of the mind, and not
 acquiring the habit of reading and study;
And attempting to compel others to believe and live as we do.

Now let's try to weave these insights into one accord. To do so, I return to the Hindu image of Indra's net, which we discussed earlier. If you recall, Indra's net is infinite. It holds all of life together and consists of a clear jewel at each knot, and each jewel contains and reflects all the others. We mentioned how each of us is such a jewel or knot, depending on whether our spirit is clear and radiant or filmed over by unprocessed experience. We also suggested that, just as a body is made up of organs and organs are made up of tissues, each of us, as a jewel in the larger net of life, is held together by our own net of smaller jewels or capacities. These capacities include generosity, integrity, sifting what is essential, patience, energy, clarity, loving-kindness, truthfulness, our all-embracing nature, and our gift for calmness or peace.

These smaller jewels or capacities correspond to the Buddha's Ten Perfections (those qualities that lead to awakening), and we can imagine them as cleansing agents that keep the jewel of our soul clear. And we can imagine their opposites (those shrinking qualities that lead to numbness) as those darkening agents that keep us living as a knot. In large measure, the art of living as a spirit in the world evolves from the practice of negotiating the qualities that enlarge or shrink our sense of life in any given situation. Whether we live as a jewel or a knot depends on whether we ride the rhythms that wake us or the rhythms that numb us.

The Enlargements and the Dwindlers

With this in mind, I offer the Buddha's Ten Perfections (those qualities that lead to awakening) as enlarging sensibilities paired with their opposites (those shrinking qualities that lead to numbness). I invite you to consider each pair as indicative of an ongoing tension of awakening that we are drawn into by experience in order to discern our capacities of being (living as a jewel) from the perceptual entanglements that hold us back (living as a knot). Since we are always balancing between liberating these faces of the Divine and wearing the confining masks that keep us from them, I invite you to assess where you are in each of these tensions—as a way to understand what lies before you as your own work as a Bodhisatta, as one on the path to awakening.

—— :: ——

Generosity, or *Dana-parami*, is the enlargement of who we are until we are a conduit for the flow of life, which, if opened to, will move through us as a perpetual gift. Within this spaciousness, we understand that we, at heart, feel everything but own nothing. In opposition to this sensibility, enabling distrust over trust and collecting and nurturing offenses *keep us from generosity*.

Virtue, or *Sila-parami*, is the quality of integrity by which what is inner matches what is outer, and the quality of congruence by which who we are and what we do become one. Both are maintained by the enlargement known as character, by which we act in accord with the deeper currents of life. In opposition to this sensibility, empowering anonymous judgment over the courage to stand in one's truth without judging others, and the illusion that personal gain is made up of crushing others, *keep us from virtue*.

Renunciation of all that is not essential, or *Nekkhama-parami*, is the enlargement of discerning want from need so that we practice a shedding of what is entangling. In opposition to this sensibility, refusing to set aside trivial preferences *keeps us from renunciation of all that is not essential*.

Patience within the larger flow of life, or *Khanti-parami*, is the enlargement that allows us to accept through humility that life and its currents are larger than our will. In opposition to this sensibility, the tendency to worry about things that cannot be changed or corrected, and insisting that a thing is impossible because we cannot accomplish it, *keep us from humility and patience*.

Energy, or *Viriya-parami*, is the enlargement that is possible when the charge of life force freely circulates among living things. In opposition to this sensibility, envy, wanting to be other than who we are, and emotional cowardice, not facing things, constrict our openings and *keep us from energy*.

Resolve, or *Aditthana-parami*, is the enlargement of action based on clarity. It is where intention and attention are completely one. In opposition to this sensibility, asserting indirectness over directness fuels confusion and hesitation, and these *keep us from clarity and, therefore, resolve.*

Loving-kindness, or *Metta-parami*, is the receptiveness of heart that allows us the enlargement of water, enabling us to absorb and embrace all that enters us. In opposition to this sensibility, hardening instead of staying vulnerable *keeps us from loving-kindness.*

Truthfulness, or *Sacca-parami*, is the bare experience of things as they are. In opposition to this sensibility, hiding instead of facing things and lying instead of crying *keep us from truthfulness.*

Wisdom, or *Pañña-parami*, is the all-embracing view of life beyond an individual self. In opposition to this sensibility, relentless self-pity and neglecting the development and refinement of the mind-heart *keep us from wisdom.*

Equanimity, or *Upekkha-parami*, is the enlargement of calmness, poise, and peace that becomes available when we can detach and let go of the myriad compulsions that living engenders. In opposition to this sensibility, unabated attachment and frustration *keep us from equanimity and peace.*

Certainty and Clarity

Along the way, we stumble into lighted pockets of knowing that are compelling. But attempting to compel others to believe and live as we do leads us away from any of the enlargements, as it preoccupies us with a false and endless task that erodes the qualities of being awake. In truth, certainty is often mistaken for clarity. For certainty fixes knowledge like a photograph of a stream, while clarity is the awakened ability to apprehend precisely whatever part of the living stream is flowing before us.

The dwindlers at work in us retreat into certainty, always trying to fix or freeze what we know, while the enlargements reveal themselves through clarity, always trying to restore immediate living.

So in your days, when feeling narrow and needing to broaden, when feeling less and needing to deepen, put down what seems certain and reach for what seems clear. Know you are a sun rising and falling along a tenuous horizon, like all the suns before you, strung between forces that both enlarge and shrink your sense of life. It is a beautifully difficult set of tensions that only those blessed to be alive can experience. Like hot notes on timeless strings, we are music fingered by the gods.

Breaking Patterns

We go into change rehearsing the history
that brought us to this point.
❖ *Parker Palmer*

Often we have to rehearse the truth until we find the courage to
live it. In this, repetition is not failure, but the heart's way to learn
how to be in the world. Yet like everything else of significance,
this process has an attractive yet false counterpart waiting nearby
to distract us. We can describe the repeating that is unnecessary
as the reliving of scripts, or *unconscious repeating*, and the repeating
that is necessary as the rehearsing of truth, or *conscious repeating*.
And we could say that the near enemy of rehearsing the truth is
being trapped in reliving scripts. Though the difference between
these is hard to keep in view—especially when in the throes of
either.

Nevertheless, the way an actress rehearses the situations she is
given until her character is one with the character she is playing,
the drama of life demands that we put in the effort to consciously
work with what we're given until we practice our way into
honest living. Without such effort, we lapse into unconscious
entanglements, like a dog that incessantly tangles itself in its leash.
And as such a dog will push its ball out of reach and whine and
pout, we can nudge the truth of who we are beyond the reach

of our self-created limitations and whine and pout and grow sad. In this way, when we repeat our reactions to living and not our attempts to live, we find ourselves trapped.

In contrast, Paula Underwood Spencer wisely states, "If you want to be truly understood, you need to say everything three times. Once for each ear, and once for the heart." The implication is that things that are worth experiencing and communicating have to be repeated in order to grasp and share the fullness of their meaning. We must enter them more than once, receive them more than once, articulate them more than once, and listen more than once. This brings us back to rehearsing the truth. So when something is working you and you've only barely spoken of it, don't limit your growth because you have no one else to talk to. Find a willing stranger and make a new friend. The growth of our soul demands that we break all hesitation.

When feeling the press of the patterns that govern our lives, these distinctions are muddy. Often, it is a slow and unclear process to move from unconscious repeating to conscious rehearsing. But this slow clarifying is part of self-transformation. The process is powerfully distilled by Portia Nelson in her poem, "Autobiography in Five Short Chapters":

I walk, down the street.
   There is a deep hole in the sidewalk.
I fall in
I am lost . . . I am helpless.
   It isn't my fault.
It takes forever to find a way out.

I walk down the same street.
   There is a deep hole in the sidewalk.
   I pretend I don't see it.
   I fall in again.
I can't believe I am in the same place.
    But, it isn't my fault.
It still takes a long time to get out.

I walk down the same street.
   There is a deep hole in the sidewalk.
   I see it is there.
   I still fall in . . . it's a habit.
    My eyes are open.
    I know where I am.
   It is my fault.
   I get out immediately.

I walk down the same street.
   There is a deep hole in the sidewalk.
   I walk around it.

I walk down another street.

So breaking patterns involves repeating. There is no getting around it, though we are always pressed to discern whether we are reliving what doesn't work or peeling away of what is false. In addition to this, we are frequently swimming like salmon against the current of a disposable society that discourages us from looking at anything more than once. It reminds me of the lonely woman and the second flower. In early spring, she is stopped by a burst of sun on a peony on the north side of the city. A few days later, she sees another peony in her friend's yard. But she thinks, "I've seen this flower before." And so she doesn't pay attention. But it is the second flower that holds a secret for her. Pretty soon, she thinks life is repeating, when all that is repeating is her want for a flower she's never seen.

The truth is that breaking out of cycles is an archetypal passage that everyone who ever lived has had to face. Consider the Viking myth of Kalavalah. Here we find a woman who is under the spell of a wizard. For nine hundred years, she is bejeweled constantly and dresses solely to please him. One day, as he bids her to put on yet one more thing to please him, she begins to undress, breaking the spell. Soon, she stands before him naked, saying, "This time not for you, but for me." As she turns away, free for the first time in almost a thousand years, she becomes a salmon and, shimmering, swims upstream into her destiny.

This luminous story says a great deal about breaking patterns. It carries the challenge we each must face at some point in our lives: When do we stop dressing for others? When do we stand naked and declare, "This time . . . for me." If we refuse this challenge, we end up under a spell, serving the wrong god. And more deeply and to the point: Who is the wizard we serve? What is the spell? What constitutes our undressing?

Sometimes the wizard is our insecurity, which wants us to dress larger than we are. Sometimes it is our want to be loved, which wants us to do or say anything to be accepted. Sometimes it is our fear, which wants us to stay in hiding from all that life has to offer. Whatever the manner of demand, whether imposed by others or self-created, the wizard is a false master who can distract us for a thousand years. And serving the wizard, the weak won't break from being weak but from a shyness of God. What's left, it seems, is to strike one's mind in hopes of breaking, not into smaller portions of the self, but into a more fundamental, organic whole. Until one rainy day, while riding the same train to work, we chance to watch the back of another person's head, only to realize once again in our rediscovered nakedness that there is no wizard. There is only the miracle of this moment that we have rehearsed our way into.

In the Middle of the Path

To love everything is like a fire.
When love is done, all that's left
is God and the path.

❖ *George quoting Angeles quoting Rumi*

Once broken open, there is no turning back. Once the heart unlocks, it gasps and cries like a newborn at this thing called air. It is miraculous and painful to be so sensitive, to feel everything, to register everything, to have everything leave its mark. So, once alive, inside and out, how do we do this?

It is a great source of humility that the wonder and the breaking happen all at once. The flutist weeps after finally playing Debussy at the same instant the lost boy from the Sudan dreams of his village burning over and over. That I can stare with you into the breach between the endless love and the endless suffering, take your hand, and listen to your damaged heart is a privileged ride. Just what has life done to us?

The mountains endure another day of pilgrims dancing and mourners pulling at their faces and another night of animals chewing grasses from the cracks in their ancient stone. And legend has it that, after the ash had cooled and they came back into what had been Pompeii, they found, hardened into a column, in the middle of a path, what must have been a person. The figure's mouth was permanently open, eyes all done with their seeing, arms and legs frozen in mid-movement. It was impossible to tell if, in their searing moment, this person had been running or dancing.

Either way, we have only this chance to love—now, today, to love whoever or whatever is before us. For the mountains will outlast us. The love will outlast us. But who we are will be used up to keep the blessing going. So put down whatever you have carved that is sharp—your mind, your edge, all your prepared responses. This is something that beggars all preparation. In the loving, nothing is ever saved and nothing is ever lost.

Movement 3

Inner Courage and Where It Lives

The Interior Blessing

Being who you are is a prayer.
❖ *the abstract artist Grazyna Wolska*

The inlet is most happy being rushed by the sea. Imagine the exchange of waters. In just this way, our core, the center of our being, is our inlet to God. It is where the soul can spill into the greater sea of Spirit and where Spirit upon return can cleanse a single soul. For us, love opens the inlet and fear closes the inlet. So standing by one's core involves the courage to inhabit this inlet. In fundamental ways, the rush of all-there-is coming and going cleanses and shapes who we are. This is the interior blessing.

What does this blessing—this cleansing and shaping, this rush of things coming and going—look like in a life walking on earth? Imagine a Native American warrior bowing so the boil of his heart can clear his head and rush into the Great Spirit that lives in the earth. Or a policeman closing his eyes at the symphony, letting the strings replace the sound of guns replaying in his mind. We are each a walking inlet, trying to exchange our being with the world.

Often, the press of extreme circumstance reveals the interior blessing. One compelling example is Dietrich Bonhoeffer, the Lutheran pastor imprisoned for his part in a failed assassination attempt on Adolf Hitler. In October of 1944, as the Allied troops marched further into Germany, the Nazis executed more and more prisoners. It was during these days that Bonhoeffer was moved with others from Flossenburg prison to a Gestapo detention cellar on Prinz Albrecht Strasse in Berlin. From his hellish cell, Bonhoeffer wrote his last poem, amazingly entitled, "By Kindly Powers Surrounded." It was from there that he wrote his fiancée, Maria von Wedemeyer, with extraordinary peace, "I sense my connection with you all. It's as if, in solitude, the soul develops organs of which we're hardly aware in everyday life . . . I live in a great unseen realm of whose real existence I'm in no doubt." Shortly after writing this, just three weeks before the Allied troops liberated Berlin, Bonhoeffer and his co-conspirators were prodded naked from their cells and paraded to a makeshift gallows where, on April 9, 1945, they were hung.

Just where does the strength of this connection come from? Estrus Tucker, a teacher in Fort Worth, Texas, devoted to strengthening the esteem and spirit of troubled youth, says simple courage, anonymous courage, is born out of love. For it is love that enables us to reach through our cloud of fear to pull each other back into the light. From outside the feeling of that love, actions seem monumental, even incredible. But to those compelled by their love, what is required is obvious—not special or worthy of medals, just inevitable. Necessary as breathing or eating. Courage born out of love feels like that. And standing by one's core is also born out of love, an unmitigated love of life. It feels as inevitable. This, too, is the interior blessing.

Let me tell you about a fourth-grade teacher in an unsafe neighborhood in Boston. On the third day of shooting outside the school, she found two of her little ones crouched on the floor of her classroom trying to solve their math problems. She knelt over them and held them. What kind of math did they learn that day? What did they take away about how things add up? When she walked them home, the smaller child's mother thanked her through the screen door, "You didn't have to go out of your way." The teacher turned, her heart swirling in the inlet, and two blocks away thought, "My job is to find something to love in every child." All of this—her holding the girls, her walking them home, her resolve to find love between the bullets—all of this is the blessing manifest by standing by one's core.

While it helps to talk separately about the sea of Spirit and the sea of the world in order to perceive them better, they do not appear separately in our days. The same is true about our need for courage in the inner dimension and out in the streets. As soon as we start to tell stories like the woman teaching math in the midst of gunfire or of the Lutheran pastor who returned to Germany in 1937 to resist national socialism, we start to see how the interior blessing is only a blessing if we can find the love and courage not to hide it from the world.

Now we start to enter the realm of inspired leadership. By this, I do not mean the direction of armies or the passing of much-needed legislation. More, I admire and long for the quiet, constant courage that lets the timeless, nameless Spirit rinse through the inlet of our core *into* the world. We wait for rain to cool things off and to help things grow, the way we wait for God to save us. But letting Spirit cleanse the world through the inlet of our being is how God waits within for us to release Him through our love. This is the interior blessing, which, brought to light, can irrigate the world.

The Secret Life of Detail

Loving is the highest form of knowing.
⋄ *Parker Palmer*

It was watching him build a boat in our backyard. I was seven, and my father had all the quiet intensity of Noah, sanding a wooden hull before dawn. I would wake and hear the rub of sandpaper in the distance. When I bent the blinds to take a look, there he was, a cup of coffee steaming, pipe hanging from his mouth, the stars fading, the light coming up. He never seemed as happy. It made me feel that something important was coming.

Even as a boy, my father had this romance with boats. In Brooklyn during the Depression, he'd skip lunch and use his milk money to find a way to Prospect Park, where he'd watch older men sail their model sloops. It wasn't long before he built his own.

I remember hearing him at night, downstairs with his tools. He could remake the world in wood. After he finished building his thirty-foot ketch, he took to reading about famous sailing ships. He'd find their plans and scale them down. And then, a journey of detail began that took months, as he would build, plank by tiny plank, a half model—exact in size and scale.

Sometimes I'd sit on the steps to the basement and watch. It was his immersion and intense focus that gripped me. This was more than discipline. This was entering another world through the doorway of detail. Somehow, I could see that every detail had to be considered and attended, if the magic was to show itself. As if he could attend a piece of wood into telling its story. As if the wood could be loved into softening its hardness long enough for him to shape it as he wanted. Once I watched him use a tweezer to place a deadeye the size of a pin into place near a tiny mast, and, in that moment, he seemed to feel the entire history of ships at sea. I could tell by his face.

It is only some forty years later that I realize the secret of detail my father gave me. For it is our thoroughness of attention that opens the life that is teeming in things. A thoroughness which often requires us to bow our head and open our hands, a humble giving over that asks us to be caringly precise. He didn't know he was teaching it. I didn't know I was learning it. But this was my first lesson as a poet.

We forged different things from the fire, to be sure, but we worked from the same source. I don't know if he ever knew this. But I understood his life more fully from a distance, because I pored over every detail of my father when he wasn't looking: the way the corner of his mouth would twitch before he'd tell a joke, the way his lips would move ever so slightly when lost in reading, the way he would slightly stammer when coming close to something that made him feel vulnerable. I loved him and knew him the way he loved his boats.

So now, when feeling lost, I know to look at anything, long enough till I stop assessing it and start pouring my attention into it. I keep looking until my love relaxes it open, the way the sun undoes a bud. I keep looking till I feel the ache of being alive flow from me into it. Then I try to pay attention until the world's delineations that say we are separate melt away. I pay attention further and pour my care and curiosity into every edge. This is the secret life of detail, the secret that binds us. Oh, it may lead to accomplishment or excellence. But the real secret is that, like aligning the tumblers of an ancient lock hidden in the center, it is our complete immersion into the nearest, smallest thing—attention let go until it turns into love—that unlocks the flood of Oneness waiting.

Our Fierce Impulse to Live

From a spiritual perspective, attachment is the complex of
dynamics that bind our capacity for love to self-centered
desires. The root of the word, a-*tache*, means *nailed to*.
Spiritual traditions see attachment as nailing our capacity
for love to something other than what it was meant for.
∴ *Gerald May*

At first, our fierce impulse to live is bent on survival, fending
off events and each other. But then, by some ever-shifting miracle, our stubbornness is broken, and we are moved, if blessed,
through that primitive survival into a deeper reality in which
our lives depend wholly on each other, the way blood relies on
organs to keep it flowing.

A complex journey stands between our primitive want to
survive and this more humble recognition of how everything is
connected. That journey takes many of us through the purging
of our attachments. Or, as Gerald May so powerfully puts it, we
must live through the nailing of our capacity to love to certain
ideas, people, and things.

Just how does attachment start? It's hard to say, but I know,
for me, like many, it began when as a boy my want to live and
my want to be loved became confused. Pretty soon, I nailed my
sense of survival to the idea that life was only possible if in love.
When love relationships failed, I grew desperate to make them

work, to make them last, until I gave myself away as kindling to keep the fire of life as I imagined it going.

Often, our personal forms of attachment grow out of painful situations that we spend much of our lives trying to correct. My mother was an angry person. She seethed and smoldered much of the time. It was like living near a volcano, never sure when it might erupt. I'm not sure what painful situation she was reacting to. But I quickly learned how to absorb her heat and threw my attention on her like water. But it was never enough. There was always more fire than I had water. And even when leaving home, I looked for fires to put out, thought this was love. I became attached to the idea and kept thinking, "If I could only find more water."

Once our fierce impulse to live is nailed to what we want or think we want, that fierceness keeps us from the direct joy of living. And feeling cut off, we work harder and longer at getting what we want. If worked at hard enough and long enough, our attachment can deepen into addiction—that is, we can make a god of attachment. In fact, we could say that addiction is a collapse of attention by which we pursue one thing repeatedly, as if that one thing will give us everything, as if that one thing sucked on enough will take away the pain of living.

Whatever the object of such focus—alcohol, drugs, love, sex, success, money, the thrill of adventure, or the tumble of crisis—addiction is attachment run wild until, like a self-replicating Midas, everything we touch turns into our troubled self. Ironically, addiction attaches to everything in its path, nailing our troubled self everywhere we go, when all we want is to lead our self out of its trouble.

Yet the skin between reverence and addiction is thin and always near. It is humbling that we can so easily aim for one and land in the other. When attached, we can become preoccupied with one thing (the touch of a loved one or a painful image of ourselves that we need to drown) until it prevents us from being touched by anything. When we can let go of our self-interest and simply lean into our capacity to love, we can be surprised by a tender strength that appears for caring openly for the smallest thing (a wave breaking or a stranger laughing) until it becomes a doorway to everything.

Because of this tenuous turn, we must make sure that we are not misusing our attention and nailing our capacity to love to what our fear thinks will save us. A compelling example of this comes from the work of Dr. Raymond Moody, the leading authority on *the near-death experience*—a phrase he coined in the late seventies. He recounts the story of a fundamentalist minister who was in a severe car accident. Very close to death, the minister had an out-of-body experience. While he lay bleeding in the ambulance, his spirit seemed to hover alongside the siren, watching his tangled body barely tethered to his life. In a sense of time that defies words, he was thrust into a life review while following the ambulance. More than revisiting memories, he seemed to enter actual moments of his life as they were happening, as if all time keeps happening at once.

There he was, early in his determined ministry, forbidding sin and preaching hell in a fiery way. But on this particular Sunday, in this particular congregation, he saw himself behind the pulpit. From outside himself, he was stopped by how vicious he seemed. Then he focused on a nine-year-old boy listening intently and entered him, merged with him. Once inside the boy, he could feel the fear, even terror, which he had induced. He could somehow feel both at once: his obsession with striking a fear of God into others and the fear he had triggered.

When he awoke in the hospital, still alive, tubes running from his nose and arms, he was broken of all determination. Everything was different. When interviewed years later by Dr. Moody, the minister admitted, "I was surprised to learn that God was not interested in my theology, but my capacity to love."

It seems that compassion is only possible when we dare *not* to nail down our capacity to love. Only when letting our impulse to live flow without preference or judgment—in essence, loving everything—can all skins of separation vanish, at least for the moment. In this way, when I am hurtful or cold or vengeful, I can feel at once both my striking out *and* the hurt it causes—as if I'm doing this to myself. Likewise, when I am giving or listening or loving, I can feel at once both my ache to care *and* the comfort it stirs—as if I'm doing this to myself. This is the mystery of compassion at the core of all the spiritual traditions: when we dare to open our hearts to life as it happens, we *are* doing all this to ourselves. For the gift of compassion, entered without hesitation, is that we are humbled by the truth that—despite our separate bodies and personal histories and all the nailing down—we *are* each other.

It is both troubling and freeing to realize that everyone is born with a fire within that we try to ignite by rubbing our hearts against the things of the world. The feel of the fire coming up from within is what we call passion. The rubbing of our hearts against the things of the world is the purpose of experience. When we are centered in our capacity to love, the friction of experience ignites our fire; and the edge and lick of its flame is curiosity and wonder, and the fire is illuminating. When we are divided and nailed to our desires, we simply burn up. We are capable of both and often shine and burn by turns. The gentle love of everything makes a life of being lighted, while the pitfalls of attachment and addiction make burning up a way of life. A thin edge of grace often separates the two. Often, we need each other to pull us out of burning up. The mystery is that, while burning, we can still love. While burning, we can let love in. When the love overcomes the burn, we somehow cease being eaten by the fire and are warmed by the fire. In these blessed moments, or moods, or even days, we stop looking for love and become love. We cease being lighted and become light.

The Art of Facing Things

If each wound faced is a letter in God's name,
how many form the secret language we need?

I have died and come back, and it has only allowed me to ask
questions I would have otherwise feared. Along the way, I have
been encouraged, humbled, and amazed at how insurmountable
it always seems to face the simplest thing, which, upon approach,
seems anything but simple. Yet—once faced, once spoken, once
questioned in the open—the dangerous leap was only a step.
Almost always, what I feared would rip me apart, rip us apart—
once voiced, once faced—only brings us closer. Inevitably, on
the other side of these simple but difficult moments, my strong
opinions evaporate, my angers turn to sadness, and my sadness
shows itself as the carrier of my questions.

What I have had to face are the great ordinary things that all
of us have to face: the prospect of dying without having truly
lived and the prospect of living without having truly loved. The
rest are branches from these deep roots. And no one has ever
been able to figure these out alone. Or having found something
to follow, none of us can handle these alone.

I've come to recognize that there is a power in facing things,
which stems from bearing witness. When we can bear witness
to where we've been and where we are—facing and lifting
what is before us into the open—it allows everyone involved to

approach Wholeness and thereby mend. Such bearing and lifting and facing makes the past less repeatable. It keeps the past from writing our actions. It does not dissolve our wounds but lets them heal. It does not eliminate difficulties but undoes our attachment to them. It does not by itself repair who we are but erases our illusions, which entangle us away from love and truth. In this way, the sheer act of facing things and bearing witness is liberating.

As I keep exploring the question, "Where does inner courage live?" the two paths that have shaped this book—the inner effort to stand by one's core and the outer effort to face things—keep knitting together. In a surprising yet obvious way, the two keep informing each other. While each has its skillful means, together they point to a living practice whereby we reestablish our place in the world. The way that birdsong at first light helps birds to locate themselves and each other—in essence remapping their place in the world each day—so do we locate ourselves daily by the voicing and interplay of standing by our core and by engaging the art of facing things.

Each time I muster the fortitude to face a truth about life, about myself, about the messy complexity of relationships I live in, it enables me to stand more soundly and clearly by my core. In turn, each time I inch closer to my core, my ability to see and face things in the world deepens, strengthens, and clarifies. And so on. This dynamic is how we know where we stand and what is possible between us. This is where the life of courage leads.

Much of this book has tried to illuminate the advantages of standing by our core and facing the truth. But there has always been a cost for living near the truth, and we must face this squarely, too. It begins as a loneliness that arises from being misunderstood, and, depending on how lively we are in living what we know, this cost can inflame into exile, arrest, persecution, and even death. In the history of facing things, the lineage of such souls is painful and inspiring. Consider Nelson Mandela, Rosa Parks, Gandhi, Dietrich Bonhoeffer, Vincent Van Gogh, Walt Whitman, Abraham Lincoln, Sir Thomas More, Galileo, Michelangelo, Jesus, Buddha, Moses. Consider the stonemason Socrates, who challenged people to inquire into the truth of their lives and then change their lives accordingly. His courage and straightforward questioning cost him his life, so frightened are we to face ourselves. Still, the cost of not standing by our core and facing the truth is withering into a living death, which for many of us is unbearable.

Our ordinary brush with all this is often less dramatic, but no less painful or inspiring. As cancer boiled me down to what is essential, I began to shine with a rawness of spirit that somehow frightened those who had been close. There was no going back. I had been transformed beyond my will. So I awoke on the other side, closer to the pulse of things. My new loneliness began as those I loved, those who had helped to save my life, began to push me away. In quiet, cold ways, I was ushered into an unacknowledged exile. Since surviving cancer had knit us together so deeply, their casting me out ripped tissue from my heart.

Facing this has been a long process. But I have begun to understand. For so long I felt cut off. All the lifelines were cut, snapped, thrown in my face. It's taken years for me to see that there was a storm about us all. It churned us up and spit us out. It turned us around and almost drowned us. And when it hit, yes, some in their fear cut the lines themselves. But others were holding as dear as I when the lines simply snapped. Some were tangled and pulled under. And the swirl of water in their lungs made them crazy. Made some crazy to be alive. Made some crazy never to go near anyone who was caught in the storm ever again. Now I can see the force of the storm, the way it hit, closer to my side of things. It was no one's fault. They were all thrown west. And I to the east. Now I'm reminded, how big the storm, how small we are, how big the sky, the sea, the earth with its rising mountains. I understand. It was no one's fault. Still it smarts, it hurts, when thinking of those who cut the line, even out of fear. For them, I have less sympathy. Why did I not see it? There was a storm. It's cleared or moved on. And no one is to blame. I've burned the ends of the rope where it split and inhaled its smoke, while saying their names.

And years from it all, I think we loved so blindly, every one of us meaning to explore the other's face, but knocking over everything in the way. Now each of us broods, building dark images of what we think happened. I heard a song today that played when we were young. It made me ache to have them all near, just for a long minute in which none of us could speak.

Facing things is often slow going. For truth moves like an Eastern monk begging; one small step for each thing given, while the rest of the world rushes by. You see, much of what we need to face is obvious and its impact is fierce. Yet we often turn away. When a fire spreads through the mouth of our home, we find the urgency to put it out. But when fear spreads its lies like a fire, we often pretend that nothing is happening.

Still, for all of it, we have to keep standing and facing, keep crossing out of our loneliness, keep making new friends. I have a new friend. She suffers, at times, from amnesia of her true self. But when I stand by my core and face her, without any agenda, just putting who I am out there, I think it helps to jar her back into what matters most. It certainly is not my job to remind her of who she is, but simply to be who I am. And when being who you are causes someone close to remember who they are—well, that's love. Then, as I drift from all I know, I wait for her to face me so I can remember who I am. This is facing life together.

So let no one tell you otherwise. It takes courage to look. It takes time to see. Courage and time. Ask Louis Pasteur as he studied silkworms for twenty-two years until he created the first vaccines and solved the mysteries of rabies, anthrax, and chicken cholera. Or Monet as he painted his *Water Lilies* through twin cataracts. Or Buddha just after he rose from sitting through many lifetimes under the Bodhi tree. It takes courage and time to soften our eyes so that we can feel what we see. Courage to remove what stands between us, and time to let what remains touch us and change us. So give me soft eyes and a willing heart. Give me the sight that waits beneath all seeing, so I can know the compassion that waits beneath all feeling, and enter the sense of Oneness that waits beneath all thinking.

The Work of Self-Return

We are asleep with compasses in our hands.
✣ *W. S. Merwin*

There was a little boy. He and his mother were dealing with the loss of his father, her husband. He went silent in his grief for months. She grew concerned and brought him to a program called *Children to Children*. After weeks of more silence, the little boy picked up a play sword and told his mother to lie down. These were his first words since his father had died. He then thrust the sword at her and said, "You're dead." She lay there heartbroken, but kept quiet. After a time, he pulled the sword back and said, "You're alive." He kept repeating this—sword in, sword out—as his mother cried. Somehow, in his little-boy wisdom which defied words, he was practicing the journey back to life.

Like the Guatemalan girl who suffered her parents being killed by soldiers, who was found pulling the wings off a butterfly, muttering, "Poor little one," like that little girl who was torn herself, this little boy thrust the sword of grief that had pierced him "into" his mother. But for some reason, he was able to pull the sword out. This is the work of self-return, the atom of resurrection: to pull the sword out, to stop doing what has been done to us, to stop replaying how we've been hurt.

I'm not sure what happened in the quiet of his little heart, while the sword was "in" his mother, that made him realize he could pull the sword out. But we need this knowledge, again and again. I'm not sure we can teach this, which is why we need stories to help us return. In Hebrew *Haggadah* means *telling*—in particular, telling the story of the liberation of the Jews from slavery in Egypt. It can be understood as the telling of any story of liberation from bondage, internal as well as situational.

In truth, the work of self-return is a never-ending story of liberation, which bears constant telling. For we return to our core through stories more than opinions, through questions more than principles. When we offer opinions, we often surface conclusions, and, frequently, these conclusions are not even our own. Mostly, our opinions try to compensate for our failed attempts to order life. This is not worth returning to, as it tends to lead us down a maze of perceptions that seem real but which have no substance. And so our conclusions are seldom life sustaining. They often lead us away from what matters. When we listen for stories, our teachers surface: like the Guatemalan girl and the boy with the sword of grief. Through stories, such as these, we invoke direct evidence of the sacred. This evidence is often messy, not neatly tied up, but paradoxical and troublesome. But it is worth returning to, as it can help us restore what matters.

No one can blame the little girl or boy for how the pain of living spilled over and through them like an unexpected surf. But the longer we live, the more accountable we are. While regrettable, tearing the wings off the first butterfly is understandable. But how many butterflies must be torn before we stop? Together, the little girl and the little boy offer a great lesson. There is much we can forgive in the press of that first moment of pain. But if we refuse or can't learn to pull the sword out, we become pain itself and are dangerous to others.

Having been the wings torn and the one tearing the wings, having thrust the sword at loved ones and having been so thrust at, I have compassion for those who struggle to break out of patterns that have governed their whole lives—but not when people begin hurting others in order to keep their lifelong patterns intact.

Though we often deny it, we are all in this together. And no one wants to admit: it is our suffering that awakens us to the many ways we hold the gun. If blessed, we return in the middle of an argument, undone once on our knees by the light on our enemy's lip. Or while sharpening our knife, we cut ourselves, and the trickle of blood stains our list of grievances. What if pain, the kind that opens a fist, is really the tap of an angel saving us from ourselves?

Burning the Raft

Since the house is on fire, let us warm ourselves.

❖ *Italian proverb*

It is said that somewhere in his journey, Buddha came upon a river too deep and wide to cross by himself. So he stopped to build a raft out of branches, leaves, and roots to carry him to the other side. As he continued on his way, he carried the raft on his back until the ground lost the smell of water. It was then he felt the weight of the raft on his shoulders. And so he stopped carrying what had brought him to the other side, as it had become a burden. He carefully set it afire and with gratitude watched it burn. Buddha would later speak about our need to leave the things we carry that no longer serve a purpose. He even spoke of his own teachings in this way, warning his students not to be burdened by the weight of his lessons once they found themselves awakened on the other side.

Of course, this is difficult because we often grow to love what has helped us on our way. But if we carry the raft when there is no water, we grow to resent what has meant so much to us. Better to burn it with reverence as an altar to the journey. Better to carry it in our heart than useless on our back.

The Mayans of South America sustain this wisdom in a ritual known as the Fire Circle. Elders gather to sustain the fire in the center by throwing things in that need to be burned. It is a tribal way of recycling what has served its purpose.

However, there is a crucial difference between gratefully burning what no longer works and coldly discarding what is still living because we don't have the patience to care for what has cared for us. This points up how imperative it is to face ourselves, so we might live out of an honesty that knows the difference. Otherwise, we can easily think we are emulating Buddha burning his raft when we are, in fact, being ruthless and betraying the relationships that have sustained us. What good is our arrival if we litter the path with holy things prematurely burned? With the blink of our heart, we can slip from pilgrim to predator, if we are not careful—that is, full of care.

This leads us to another aspect of burning the raft—an interpersonal one. It has to do with whether we give ourselves away or not, with whether we define ourselves externally or internally. Liberating ourselves in this way depends on the courage to burn what keeps us from discovering our inner authority.

There is a story I heard my grandfather's brothers tell after a Seder in Brooklyn. They heard it in Rumania. In it, the mystic seer of a village is no longer valued by a powerful young rabbi who has taken over the leadership of the village. Deftly, the young rabbi undermines the seer's impact on the community. Though the seer has been revered as a zaddik (a holy man), the young rabbi asks the mystic not to stand out from his brethren. For the good of the community, the powerful young rabbi asks the zaddik to deepen his humility by sitting quietly in the back of the temple.

The seer is deeply hurt. Though he feels misunderstood, he doesn't want to be perceived as not being humble, and so he struggles to accept his new role. All the while, he feels strongly that he should stand up for what he was born to do. And yet, he thinks: "Which is more important—to see God or to be seen as a seer of God?" Sensing the mystic's ambivalence, the young rabbi offers to listen to all the zaddik has to say. In one of those conversations, the holy man grasps, in a glimpse of hard clarity, that the young rabbi is merely pretending to listen. Just as he is about to ask the rabbi to reconsider, it becomes apparent to the zaddik that his position in the temple is already gone.

As the rabbi leans forward to placate him, the holy man realizes that as long as he clings to what has already changed, he gives the young rabbi power over his soul. This realization is at once painful and liberating. The zaddik knows what he has to do. He takes the prayer shawl from his neck and gives it to the rabbi, thinking: "Only by burning what is no longer real, though it is dear to me, can I free myself from the tyranny of those who would try to withhold what is sacred."

As the rabbi fingers the prayer shawl that has been handed down for generations, the zaddik speaks calmly, "I no longer want what has been taken." In his remaining years, the zaddik sits quietly in the back of the temple, though it is often mistaken for the front, as the people of the village still find their way to his side to ask what he can see.

The liberating effect of this sort of acceptance—of grasping things exactly as they are and not as we wish them to be—is captured as well in an ancient Zen story. A monk is confronted by a brutish samurai, who demands that the monk reveal the secret of life. But the monk, in meditation, ignores the samurai. After repeated threats, the samurai summons all his will, "Don't you know that I could run you through in a second without blinking an eye?" And the monk, without looking up, responds, with all his surrender, "And don't you know that I could be run through in a second without blinking an eye?" The stunned warrior bows and withdraws.

Both stories speak to our need to find a place of inner authority from which we can stand in the world while rooted in the true nature of things, empowered with all its fragility and endurance. It is compelling to realize that a threat is only powerful when we cling to what is threatened. You can't be blackmailed if you have nothing to hide. You can't be indentured to success if you are content with what you have. The rabbi only has power over the zaddik if the holy man believes that who he is and what he knows can be taken away. And the samurai only has power over the monk if the monk believes that running from death will keep him from dying.

These issues press us daily. They surface in the many ways we compromise our authentic self—in order not to lose love, in order not to be rejected, in order not to lose our job security. The deft rabbi and the brutish samurai appear in many forms—as a dominant parent or partner, as an arrogant boss, or as our own worrisome nature afraid of living. In truth, we waste so much time and care guarding things that we have no control over or that are already gone. How many times do we catch ourselves suppressing what we know to be true because our position in the village is threatened, or because the brutish samurai in our life threatens to hurt us if we don't do his bidding? How much of ourselves do we give away when those we love threaten to withhold their love, or when those incapable of love threaten to extinguish our care?

This practiced ability to give up our fear of losing what we strive for is very elusive and yet necessary if we are to live authentically. In a compelling way, it frees us to live fully and unencumbered. Hard as it is, when we can stop carrying around the raft of the past (like the zaddik) and the raft of the future (like the monk), we are liberated into the Stream of Now, which connects us to everything—the way that diving into any part of the ocean, we are touched by the entire ocean. Once there, the power of the Universe supports us the way the entire current lifts a fish swimming to the surface.

All this uncovers our need to be touched by what is living and to recover from the habits that distance us from our inner authority. Just as crucial, we need to recover from the ways we guard these habits. Otherwise, we are close, but not really alive.

It seems that, sooner or later, everyone must face the need to build a raft and then the need to burn it once awakened on the other side. And it's true—no one can do this for you. Yet tell me of the things you carry that no longer serve a purpose, and I'll confess my fears of losing what I'm striving for. But why, you ask, can't we leave the raft for others? Because building our own raft of teachings is part of the crossing.

Giving Up What No Longer Works

Sometimes snakes can't slough. They can't burst their old skin.
Then they go sick and die inside the old skin, and nobody ever
sees the new pattern. You need a real desperate recklessness
to burst your old skin at last. You simply don't care what
happens to you, so long as you get out.

❖ *D. H. Lawrence*

Sacrifice originally meant *to make sacred.* As Rabbi Alan Lew tells
us, the original notion of sacrifice focused on giving up a layer
of self in order to draw closer to the transcendent. In effect, the
notion was that if you give up or shed an outer layer of skin, he
sacred can touch you. Over time, the notion of sacrifice has been
distorted to mean self-suppression or self-denial or even self-
annihilation for the love of others.

The work of true sacrifice has always been, as Saki Santorelli
says, "[t]he pull of the soul toward what is possible" once we shed
"the pull of the past toward what has been conditioned." This is
an ever-present challenge. In deep, original ways, giving up our
conditions in order that the sacred can touch us is the process of
individuation. It involves giving up layers of ego in order to be
fully touched by life. We could say that sacrifice means *giving up
what no longer works in order to stay close to what is sacred.* I've been
pursuing this notion for some time, trying to understand the lesson of it more and more deeply.

Like other things we've discussed, this is more urgent than it seems, as there is a very real danger of infection when we refuse to give up what no longer works. A compelling teacher of this is our biology. For example, when the nerve of a tooth dies, the decay can seal over itself and the tooth appears to be healing from the outside in. This can breed abscess and infection. Like all wounds, it needs to heal from the *inside out*. When the wound is discovered, dentists will try to keep it from sealing over by irrigating it. If undetected, the closed-over wound becomes a breeding ground for *unfelt decay*, which can even eat away at bone. The danger here is that such decay and infection can take place without our feeling a thing.

The parallel is sorely obvious. When we seal over our deepest pains, we become a breeding ground for infection. If never given air and never given up, our pain can decay and spread without our ever feeling it. It can even eat away at our bones. In crucial ways, the dead nerves that plague us must be sacrificed. We must give them air and give them up in order for us to feel again cleanly. This marks the beginning of healing from the inside out.

Another example comes from botany. Dr. Bruce Carlson, a leading cell biologist, tells us that at the base of every leaf is the spore of a new bud waiting to grow in its place. As long as the old leaf stays attached, the new growth is stalled, because the old leaf secretes chemicals that inhibit new growth. But once the old leaf lets go and dies, the growth inhibitors are removed, and the next leaf, a new leaf, is possible. The parallel is inwardly true. Letting the dead things that we carry fall away stops our inhibitors of growth, and this allows new things to mature in us.

Two immediate efforts can help us here. First, if we can become aware of the things we secrete that inhibit growth—like fear, distrust, resentment, envy—we can try to disempower them. But failing that, a more intuitive, almost blind courage is available by which we can directly give up what no longer works. For even if we don't understand what is actually happening, we can drop what seems dead or dying as soon as we feel it blocking or draining our sense of being alive. When holding a piece of dry ice, you don't have to understand hypothermia in order to know, pretty quickly, that you need to drop the ice.

So a key to meaningful sacrifice—to making things sacred by giving up what no longer works—is the art and practice of letting go. The great psychiatrist Gerald May found a profound instruction regarding this:

In Psalm 46, the usual translation is "Be still and know that I am God." The Hebrew for that is raphah yada eyah elohim. Raphah *is the word that gets translated as "be still or rest," but the literal meaning implies that you've been holding onto something with a white-knuckled grip, and you just let go. An ancillary meaning is "let fall." Whatever you're holding up, let it fall—and know that I am God.*

Whatever you're holding up, let it fall, let it go. Because all that is sacred is waiting below our grip. But let go of what? Of sealing over our pain and of carrying dead things. Why? To get rid of two perennial constrictions of being that never work in the long run: unfelt pain which can begin to decay and the stubborn attachment to things and feelings, the grip of which inhibits our growth.

We are all blessedly conscripted to this ancient and timeless process of sacrificing our outer layers of ego in order that the sacred can keep touching us. This endless shedding and letting go is *the work of self-return*—the return of who we are to our inborn spot of grace. All because our task in this life is to get out of the way as much as possible, so we might stretch into the power of unfiltered being, the way a small weed aches its way into the sun.

Judgment or Compassion

How do trees deal with injustice?
They grow a branch wherever they are cut.
And how do sparrows deal with grief?
They open their tiny wings and swoop
at anything that glistens. So, why am I
all cut and hungry? Because I do not
know the tree that is my soul and
refuse the sparrow in my heart.

It is one of the most difficult passages: not to turn away from injustice and not to be dehumanized by the righteousness that injustice invokes. Not to turn away from the murder or theft of a heart, a dream, a life, and not in retribution to become the murderer or thief of a heart, a dream, a life. Any of us who have been stubborn enough to achieve retribution know the satisfaction is short lived. As we care for the one soul we are given, the question becomes: is it justice or healing that we need?

We have seen what centuries of retribution in the name of justice have done. We have only doubled the number of dead. So let's put down the myth that the angel of justice needs to be blind and cold of heart in order to do her work. The reverse is actually truer: justice that is lasting is only possible through a clear eye and an open heart. The secret of justice, it seems, waits not in judgment but compassion. By compassion, I do not mean the limited view of pity, which over-sympathizes with one aspect of a situation. Rather, compassion of the deepest sort requires the difficult practice of holding as many facets of truth as possible, while feeling for all the lives involved. Justice informed by compassion reflects a maturity of heart that allows victims and perpetrators to face each other authentically. This deeper form of justice has the thief work at giving things away and the violent one dress wounds in emergency rooms.

The literal meaning of *com-passion* is *to feel with*, and we could say that the difference between whether we judge one another with a blind eye or hold each other accountable to the perennial standards of care depends on the depth to which we listen. So perhaps we need to recast our image of justice. Perhaps she needs to take her blindfold off and put her scales down. Perhaps instead she must stand between the violated and the violator with a hand on each of their hearts, deeply listening.

In truth, we start out this way. Our capacity toward compassion is innate. Consider that within seventy-two hours of birth, a baby will not cry if it hears a tape recording of its own cry, but will start crying if it hears a recording of another's cry. How can a newborn know the difference? What does such a moment of empathy tell us?

The sociologist Heinz Kohut defines empathy as "the capacity to think and feel oneself into the inner life of another person." How do we do this and what kind of world does such empathy open? When we can feel what it is to be human, and *feel with* the living, we realize that we are *in* the ocean of humanity. It surrounds us.

Yet as we grow, we often start to perch alongside of life, watching while leaning on the rail of whatever values we were taught to uphold. Before we know it, we become cold messengers whose message is muted because of our detachment. One of the lessons of quantum physics is that it returns us to the spiritual fact that we cannot separate ourselves from what we know or want to know. Experience is not out there to observe, but something vital and emerging that we are always a part of. Irrevocably, we are in relationship to everything we ask about or resist. The questions evoked by compassion reveal the fabric of those connections, while the answers provoked by judgment suppress those connections.

It was the Italian poet Petrarch who said, "It is more important to want to do good than to know the truth." That we have any hesitation about this almost seven hundred years later tells us just how great the divide is that we've created between our mind and our heart. Now we are educated to praise the fruit of one as objective and to distrust the fruit of the other as subjective, when neither instruction is helpful.

But how do we move from judgment to compassion, from blindly measuring everything on scales to listening to everything with a hand on its heart? There is a clue in the story of Petrarch (1304–1374) who, along with Dante, is considered one of the fathers of the Renaissance. In 1336, at the age of thirty-two, Petrarch set out with his brother and climbed to the top of Mont Ventoux in the Provence region of southern France, a trek of over a mile (6,263 feet). He later wrote an account of the trip. At the time, it was unusual to climb a mountain for no other reason than the experience itself, and many consider Petrarch to be the father of mountain climbing.

We can view the trek from judgment to compassion as such a climb with a loved one, done for no other reason than the experience itself. Such a path—lived in till a greater perspective is revealed—is at the heart of all embodied wisdom. So often, judgment bypasses the climb, while compassion is in the climbing with. And anyone who has climbed with a loved one to the summit of their suffering knows with Petrarch that the climb softens our stubborn judgments.

I imagine that climbing with another and *feeling with them* the difficulty in their steps is what prompted an aging poet like Walt Whitman to run back and forth in the Civil War as a medic, tending the wounded on *both* sides. I only know that *in the climb* is when I've felt the want to do good unfold into the want to be compassionate. And in climbing with others through their pain and joy, I've felt compassion unfold into a truth in which all other truths come to rest.

Once we are broken of our judgments, it becomes clear that compassionate justice is rarely just about right or wrong, but more about our courage to see and embrace the fallen part in others as the humanness in ourselves. This does not preclude holding ourselves and others accountable for the moments of trespass we engender. Rather, compassion deepens our response to such trespass, demanding that we lean into what went wrong—together. The recognition of trespass with honesty is often more helpful than unconsidered judgment that exiles the fallibility of being human.

Unconsidered and unfelt judgment often provides a way to remove ourselves from people and situations. When we feel justified in judging others, we give ourselves permission not to stay involved. It's seldom that simple. This is the hard gift of compassion, that it allows us to stay involved in a meaningful way with the living. It allows us to respond to the splendor and messiness of life.

Again, we can turn to Abraham Lincoln as a strong example of someone who responded to the messiness of life. In her article "The True Lincoln," historian Doris Kearns Goodwin discusses Lincoln's emotional strengths and recounts that:

Even as a child, he was uncommonly tenderhearted. He once stopped and tracked back half a mile to rescue a pig caught in a mire. Not because he loved the pig, recollected a friend, but "just to take a pain out of his own mind."

Lincoln seemed able to be led by his compassion and not his anxiety. And his capacity to endure his compulsions toward melancholy without thwarting his ability to respond to life under duress made him the remarkable human being that Walt Whitman praised as "the grandest figure yet, on all the crowded canvas of the Nineteenth Century."

We have all come upon something stuck in the mud by the side of the road. Most of us will stop to help. But it is important to understand why we save the mired pig. Are we hushing the symptoms of our anxiety or responding to the ache we all feel when encountering life under duress? It is hard to know the difference, for sure. But it is crucial to try and to make a practice of trying. Ultimately, the urge to hush our anxiety is not the same as facing it. Ultimately, creating noise or a list of good deeds won't keep us from ourselves or the fact that time is precious and that life will end. Isn't this at the heart of our noisy obsessions with fame and crisis? Isn't it all a way to feel important and needed? In running from the basic questions of living, haven't we become a society of firefighters whose identity of goodness so rests on putting out fires that we never face our secret life as arsonists?

Nevertheless, whatever situations we are left to mend, we all face the ache of trying to take a pain out of our mind, and the challenge of being led by our compassion and not our anxiety. Otherwise, we risk becoming all that we abhor. And if we keep setting fires with our judgment and putting them out with our guilt, the face of humanity will be scorched. This is the cost of our busy need to save each other and our righteous need to burn each other at the stake.

These dilemmas—of turning judgment into compassion, of letting vengeance disperse into forgiveness, of sinking below the noise of our anxiety till we can take a pain out of the mind— these quandaries are ageless. And our endless dream of having the courage to face our judgment, our vengeance, our anxiety, our resentments and to live with them is captured in this ancient story told to schoolchildren in India.

It is the lesson of the King Cobra, who grows the largest and lives the longest. An ordinary cobra keeps spewing venom and so becomes a feared snake. But the King Cobra doesn't bite and waste its poison. It retains, retains, and retains its venom so very patiently, with caution, in meditation for long, long years. Until the poison somehow condenses and solidifies into a diamond. The poison turned diamond is called *Nagaratinam*. When all its venom becomes a diamond, the King Cobra spits out the jewel that living has produced and dies in bliss. Dare we understand this as our purpose? I'm not brave enough to enter this alone. Still, the diamond of love waits to be crystallized in each of us.

Experiments with Love

All the arts we practice are apprenticeship.
The big art is our life.
❖ M. C. Richards

My wife Susan is a potter. She has apprenticed in an ancient form of firing that takes place in an Anagama kiln. It is an arduous form of wood-firing that is communal. It originated in Korea and migrated to Japan. In Japanese, *Anagama* means *single-chambered*. A working group of potters save their pots for months, and in the spring or fall they fire the kiln for five days straight, each shift of potters caring for the fire and raising its temperature roughly fifty degrees an hour. It takes weeks of preparation. They all cut, split, and haul six or seven cords of wood in various sizes. Then they take days to load the kiln, packing shelves tightly, but leaving more space near the floor of the kiln, so the fire will be forced to move around their unfinished wares. The fire is set and the journey takes over. With one day to go, the fire has moved to the back of the stone whale, and the cracks in its spine begin to show. Even stone will expand at two thousand degrees. Finally, the fire reaches its peak, breathing like a little sun. Then they close it up and wait for as long as they've been firing. In a week, they return and open the kiln like a tomb, not sure which of their pots will be warped or broken or seared into an artifact. But all are beautiful, with patterns of wood ash no one could design. So the potters line up, and, one at a time, they hand the still-warm pots, fired in the earth, to each other and lay them on the grass.

It is a magical process unleashed by the hard work of a small community whose artists depend on each other for weeks. Though there are legendary stories in Japan of some old master firing the Anagama kiln alone, no one can really fire alone. This is the third season of firing that Susan has been a part of. While historically women in Japan have not been allowed to enter the kiln, here there are more women than men. They are covered with soot and sweat, hot licks from the firebox. As I watch them stoke the side holes, I can hear the fire hiss.

The heat flashes on my face, and I think, we are no different than these pots waiting to be formed. We shape our hearts like clay and place them, full of hope, in the single chamber of experience. And we are just as fragile in the face of pure heat, which will bend us or crack us open. Humbled by the effort necessary to accept that however we come out after cooling in the dark, we will be beautiful and of use.

Just then, the old teacher in the group, wearing torn jeans and followed by a golden retriever named Einstein, plops down next to me, puffing his pipe. He listens to the single-chambered fire roaring inside around eight hundred pots, and his eyes light up like little coals themselves. "If you work the kiln enough, the fire talks to you. Listen. Can you hear that rumble? The fire is happy. It will grow sad in a while, and then we'll have to feed it."

My wife and her shift partner are working full blast now, timing when to stoke the side holes. They lift the flash door, and a hot red fire darts out briefly, as if from the center of the earth.

The old potter keeps talking. "It all comes from the fire. You can hear it, smell it, see it. If the center of the fire is dark, it needs more wood. It's that simple. It's the relationship with the fire that is the teacher." I am struck by this. It has always been so. The trick is to stay close enough to learn without getting burned. My hands are cold, but my throat is red from hours of watching them work with the kiln.

The old potter pokes me with his pipe. "You see that gadget on top of the kiln?" He's pointing to the digital pyrometer, whose tiny sensor is threaded into the heart of the fire. It can register up to 2,500 degrees Fahrenheit. He takes a puff. "I don't like it. It causes them to watch the gadget and not the fire."

This speaks to the distractions of modern life. What we've devised as tools, like the pyrometer, can divert us from the fire that is the teacher. We listen to voicemail rather than talk to the person. We watch the news instead of looking directly into life. Often the fire is right before us, but we miss the teaching when we look to the pyrometer to read our experience.

Susan opens the metal flash door and throws in a log of pine. The wave of heat opens our eyes. There's sweat on my lip. I know it's true—no one can fire alone. And sometimes the work of the fire—the growl and the hiss—is right before us. It warms our throats and opens our eyes. We don't need digital readouts or second or third opinions. We simply need to listen to the center of the fire and feed it—in our heart, in our soul, and in our experiments with love.

The Gateway: Acceptance

As soon as we accept life's most terrifying dreadfulness, at the risk of perishing from it . . . then an intuition of blessedness will open up for us . . . Whoever does not, sometime or other, give their full and *joyous* consent to the dreadfulness of life can never take possession of the unutterable abundance and power of our existence.

✧ *Rainer Maria Rilke*

What Rilke reports from the edge of mystery is a hard pill to swallow. But having fallen to where he was able to climb, I can only drop my shoulders in awe and confirm that it is true. He speaks of a fundamental courage *to accept what-is*. From the smallest sliver of a hurtful remark to the fact that we will die, the courage to accept what-is, is the first step to seeing what else is possible. In the martial arts, this fundamental courage to see things as they are, in the midst of experience, informs a sense of poise and readiness. When someone is coming at you aggressively, the anger with which they approach and the fear with which you might receive them can blind you to the precision of what is actually happening in that moment.

By accepting what-is in that moment, you can part the anger and fear like a veil, to see more accurately that a raised arm is coming from above and to the left, headed for your shoulder at a certain velocity. By accepting precisely what is happening, it becomes clear that the path of this attack is one stroke of motion in a vast stretch of stillness. That makes it clear that there is a great deal of space around this agitated stroke in which to move. This is the freedom of acceptance. And it applies to much larger concerns, such as pain. In our fear, it feels that pain is everywhere. But when we can find the courage to accept the fact of a particular pain, it often becomes clear that, like an unexpected aggressor, our pain is one agitated stroke in a larger stretch of stillness that is the rest of our life. This makes it possible to summon all that is not in pain to meet what is in pain.

This courage to see clearly what is before us, around us, and within us applies as well to the largest acceptance of all—that we will die. In accepting death, we can see more easily where we can live. In accepting that we have no control over the stream of life, we can see more easily the gestures we do have control of, which sages refer to as our chance to steer in the stream. In accepting that life is relentless in its rush of experience, we can see more easily where it is tender and wondrous. In facing the harsher ways of those we love, we can ask for authentic relationship and accept the hard work of how to get there.

In our modern world, acceptance is often misconstrued as resignation, as acquiescing or giving up. In actuality, as you can see, it is acceptance that makes right action possible. If you wake in a strange room, it is acceptance of all the walls that lets you find the doorway out. If you are suddenly crossing the loft of an old barn that is on fire, it is acceptance of where the planks have rotted that lets you step on the beams that remain solid. Just in this way, if you wake in a room of takers, it is acceptance of their self-centeredness that lets you find the one set of open arms that will lead you out. And when you find yourself crossing the old

barn of your past which has suddenly caught aflame, it is acceptance of what can no longer bear your weight that lets you stand
on the few solid things that will hold you up. Accepting what-is
often lets us find our way through difficulty.

Over the years, I have been broken of my stubbornness into
accepting a great many things. Though I started out trying to
fill my loneliness by chasing after others, I had to accept that
no one could find the roots in that dark hole but me. Though I
started out determined to achieve greatness as a poet, like Icarus,
the closer I got to the Source, the more it melted me back into
my humanness. And though, during my days of cancer, I wanted
to be spared from my suffering, I was humbled to lay flat on
the earth where I finally heard the fire at the center. I can only
admit that, starting out with dreams of being a great conductor,
I landed as a thorough note in hopes of being sung. And I am
happier for it.

Everywhere we turn, there is a need for some form of acceptance. For loss is not alterable. No matter what we try to do or
say, we cannot restore what is lost or mask the feelings of grief
that loss engenders. So the gateway to meaning is not in avoiding
loss or getting over loss, but in the effort *to accept what-is* while
keeping our heart open. We lose access to what is real when we
try to make something else happen that will preoccupy us or
divert us from the fact of our loss. I did this in working hard
to maintain the illusion of a friendship that meant so much to
me, when in my heart, after thirty years, I knew that our bond
had been cut. I just couldn't accept it. It was too painful. I then
plummeted inward, and it became harder to surface at all. My
refusal to accept what had happened and my inwardness about
it only made things worse. Grief will do this to us. Too often we

privatize our grief and circle each other in our personal versions of hell.

In Europe in the 1800s, those who had lost someone wore a black band on their arm to let everyone know that they were grieving. It was refreshing that this made grief public and communal. Custom was that you would do this for a year. The implication, however, was that, by the end of the first year of living without the one you lost, you should have sufficiently grieved and moved on. But ultimately, we live *through things* and *with things*. We do not *get over things*. In truth, grief rings like an echo that doesn't stop, and thins to a frequency below the normal hearing of those who have not yet grieved. The truth is that as long as we believe the goal is to *get over* such things, we will lack the inner skill of *living with* such things. And all the while, loss and grief keep thinning till they sound under our breath in the skin of our ear and in the muscle of our heart.

Our obsession with avoiding grief is the major obstacle to experiencing true freedom of the heart. At the same time, grief is the chief practice ground for acceptance. Such acceptance, not on an intellectual level, but in the belly of our days, is a way to kneel by the endless stream that runs through all of life. Whether we drop to our knees or are brought to our knees, drinking from that stream is what makes us wholehearted.

Such acceptance can cleanse us of our suffering through surrender. Such a journey leaves us humbled and compassionate while still here on earth. Often, when things are difficult, all we can do is stay true to what we feel. Often, all we can do is trust this acceptance which seems so hard to enter.

Sniffing Out What Is Sacred

Sometimes a glance, a few casual words, fragments of a
melody floating through the quiet air of a summer evening,
a book that accidentally comes into our hands, a poem or a
memory-laden fragrance, may bring about the impulse which
changes and determines our whole life.

❖ *Llama Govinda*

When I think of the times I've been lost in my life, each had the
feel of an earthquake that upended something foundational. At
the time, I was hurt, frightened, disoriented, unsure how to go
on. Yet who would have guessed that one foundation broken
apart would reveal another.

I was barely ten when I asked my parents about God. They
looked at each other and flatly shut the door, saying, "We don't
believe in God." It was the way they closed off all conversation
that made me feel orphaned in my inquiries. I felt completely on
my own. This was my first sense of death—the death of home.
But it caused me to venture further into my own firsthand experience of everything larger than me. Ironically, because of how
they shut me out, I solidified my bond with the mysteries.

As a teenager, I fell in love for the first time, and I fell deeply.
She was beautiful and had questions of her own. In my innocence, I imbued her as the keeper of all that was holy. When she
left me for another, I was devastated and darkly lost for almost

two years. But one day, when exhausted of my very colorful despair, I sat in a field, drawn to watch the bees pulling nectar from the dew-heavy flowers. I was stopped by the beauty that keeps on creating itself no matter what we experience. Here, the death of my first love had led me to the unshakable bottom of beauty.

At the age of thirty-six, in the midst of my struggle with cancer—between angiograms and MRIs—Grandma died. It was my first taste of inconsolable loss. For no one loved me like Grandma. She believed in me more than I could comprehend. And she was gone. The ground beneath me had split apart. Within months, the cancer resurfaced in a rib in my back. I felt utterly lost. It was the death of my faith. My rib was removed. When I woke on the other side, after having nothing to rely on, I discovered a deeper faith—one that exists like gravity, independent of our wishes and regrets.

It was almost ten years after cancer, when I was forty-five, that my former wife Ann and I separated after helping to save each other's lives. To my surprise, several of my deepest friends, who had held me during surgeries and chemo, cast me out. This made me question the very ground by which I enter friendship. Not only could I no longer trust those I so loved, but I could no longer trust my own assessment of closeness. I felt isolated, and what I knew that was dependable, within me and around me, was no bigger than my palm. This was a death of friendship that I am still recovering from. But it forced me to fall into the bedrock of a deeper self which sniffs out what is sacred with the wonder of an animal—independent of what others think.

Still, when forty-eight, I learned that the press that had published my epic poem *Fire Without Witness* had gone out of business. In doing so, they had destroyed almost 1,500 copies without ever contacting me. Though I was experienced enough to know that this was just an external loss, it punctured me to my core. It had taken me ten years to birth that book. It was my deepest journey into the Unconscious. Try as I did to accept this brush with impermanence, I felt defeated and grew depressed.

Months later, I was driving a rental car from Albuquerque to Santa Fe to see my good friend Wayne when the old mountains baking under the big southwest sky somehow snapped me back into life. If they could outlive native names and Spanish names and American names, I could outlive this.

Now, at fifty-five, I still miss Grandma terribly. But now her presence is foundational. She is in the silence that holds my missing rib, in the flowers waiting for the bees to find their nectar, and in my lifelong sense of God as everything larger than me. As I consider where I've been, I realize that, at every turn, I've been broken of my preferences, and so I find, to my delight, that I am interested in everything.

To Be a Clear Vessel

Some day [we] will see
the entire light of this planet
through the window of a tear . . .
❖ *Léon Felipe*

The Spanish poet Felipe is talking about the marriage of two suns—the outer light with the inner light—made visible by our courage to feel. In making light visible, compassion is an ancient tool of knowing. For in addition to being healing, compassion is revealing. We underestimate this.

The truth is, if you take the medicine of what you know and marry it to the medicine of who you are, you have the chance to become a clear vessel. But for what? For healing, for drawing the toxins out of others and discharging them where they can do no further harm. This is the ancient call of the shaman—the earliest form of healer.

It seems we have always had two choices: to run from pain or be a healer. And when, out of love, we face our pain and the pain of others—whether physical, psychological, or spiritual—the art of caring centers on the question: how do we hold pain so as not to spread it? In awe, I wonder: how do therapists listen for hours without darkening their hearts? How do doctors and nurses mend wound upon wound without dreaming of cuts? This quandary affects us all. Whether you listen to a stranger's troubles or travel the world to hold the children of war, whether you are an oncology nurse coaxing thin needles into hardened arms or a tired mother putting a bandage on your little girl's knee, the act of love has always involved absorbing another's pain. But being a healer necessitates letting go of whatever pain or toxins we absorb, before they make us ill or land with dark contagion in others.

Yet no one quite knows how to do this. This is why we take the troubles we brush up against home with us, why we replay another's pain while trying to sleep. This is why we get drawn into codependency and overthinking someone else's life. The challenges alone outline a life journey: how to be a clear vessel, how to draw the toxins from those we love, how not to hold on to them, how to discharge them safely. And if we can gather some wisdom in these regards, how do we practice it and teach it along the way without lessening our compassion?

In his classic *The History of Massage*, Robert Noah Calvert traces and weaves the many threads that form the history of touch and how massage was an early craft of the shaman. Over ten thousand years ago, the shaman was the first priest-physician who appeared as a medicine man or sorcerer, dancing, chanting, beating drums. The earliest medical records—carved in clay and written on papyrus—reveal incantations, spells, exorcisms, prescriptions, and case histories. Medicinal ingredients included fruit, cereals, spices, flowers, garlic, roses, oats, and massage plasters. An early shaman from South America would gently rub a patient with leaves, stirring the evil spirits to disappear without upsetting them. Likewise, massage was a form of cleansing by which a shaman would coerce or chase demons from the body.

Early shamans practiced massage worldwide. In fact, many travelers learned of massage in Africa and brought it back to Mesopotamia, Egypt, and Greece, but often without any knowledge of the shaman who used it. Along the way, we have separated from our understanding of how touch heals. Even now we mostly think of touch as soothing, which it is, but have lost sight of how it draws out what is ill.

Yet all the while that travelers were separating the art of touch from its healing power, the mystical lineages—both West and East—kept deepening the impact of touch on the inwardness we call Spirit or Mindfulness. This culminates in the West as the sacred ritual of anointing and in the East as the practice of compassion.

The word *anoint* comes from the Latin *inungere, to smear on.* It meant originally *to rub olive oil or essences on the body.* As Homer sang his songs throughout the countryside of Greece, he spoke of anointing in the *Odyssey* many times. Anointing also became known as a way to soften and moisturize the skin. Olive oil, perfumed with myrrh or sweetened with cinnamon, was used in early times. In ancient medicine, Hippocrates spoke of anointing the areas around a wound with a thin, folded compress that was scented with pitch. Over time, *anoint* began to gather its therapeutic meaning: to rub essences on the body, to soften and moisturize the skin, to wall off the infected areas of a wound.

Eventually, without any knowable point of transformation, the interior meaning of *anoint* evolved as *to bless a life with essence, to soften the membrane between our soul and the world,* and *to keep our wounds and our pain from spreading.* It was the ministry of Jesus that brought the laying on of hands into the personal realm of one spirit bringing the essence of its love to bear on the sickness of others. The word *Christ* itself comes from the Greek *chriein*, meaning *to anoint*. And the point of all christening, all anointing, is to consecrate, to make what we touch and hold sacred.

At the same time, the development of meditation in the East was extraordinary. The Tibetan word *tonglen* means *taking and sending*. In particular, the Tibetan Buddhist practice of tonglen can be seen as the work of the shaman approached through meditation. It is a form of anointing one suffering heart with another. The essence of the practice is to breathe in the suffering of another person and to breathe out loving-kindness, compassion, and healing.

Meditation teacher Andrew Weiss describes the practice this way:

Tonglen embodies Muktananda's teaching: in offering to help another, we help ourselves. In the face of great pain and suffering, we can exchange self and other . . . and, even if momentarily, tap into the great well of suffering and healing that arises and passes away in the vastness of human consciousness.

Though it may seem straightforward, drawing pain from others and practicing compassion is seldom easy. This is why, in living out the tensions of being human, we need to commit to the exchange of self and other. Because, just as one tide takes out so the next can bring in, part of us is inevitably involved in losing sight of how deeply we are connected. Profoundly, in answer to these tensions, the ritual of anointing and the practice of compassion have been developed over centuries as the recurring tide through which we can continue to consecrate each other. At the heart of it, the remembrance that we are each other—and that when we touch, there is no end to the touch—is at the heart of all healing. And it is just as inevitable.

It's interesting that the Japanese ideogram for *the heart of listening* is comprised of three figures entangled with each other—the ear, the eye, and the heart It suggests that engaging all three at once is what accesses wholeheartedness. It implies that a complete effort to hold and release suffering is what allows the heart to hear what life has to say.

To be a clear vessel may be the oldest of vocations through which the line between the physical and spiritual is penetrated by the courage of love to keep loving, until what we touch and hold is alleviated of its burden, at least for a while. In this way, the shaman that lives in each of us can take in and send out some of the pain which no one can avoid.

Feeling the light of the planet through a single tear makes me aspire to be a spiritual citizen. It makes me stop on the wet city street near the bus station till I sense the wind about to curl around the corner. I feel that light carrying the resin of things almost said by others miles away. I slow to inhale the breeze, accepting the pains of those I'll never meet. And like the shamans who sing in the dark, I believe that somewhere beneath my personality, beneath my goodwill, somewhere in the chemistry of spirit that enables flesh to heal, I can close my eyes and exhale the world, doing my small part to blunt the edges.

Ways of Living

How do I dress
the wound in you
that is me?

Few of us intend to be hurtful, but we often perpetrate pain on others in our insistence and passion for how we believe good needs to be done. The truth is that we are frightfully flawed, and it is only our attempts to keep loving our mistakes into pieces of the path that make any difference.

In this regard, we have these choices about how to live. As we have seen, we can remain blunt and unaware and so replay our suffering on others. Or, if blessed to be thrown into open living, we can be drawn into what we need to learn. In time, this may allow us to face ourselves and others in an effort to own our own trespasses. This is liberating and humbling. Believe it or not, the effort *not* to tear each other's wings can heal the world, if we can stand by our core and love each other until we surface our true nature. This is the work of being *vulnerable*; the word comes from the Latin word *vulnus*, which means *the ability to carry a wound gracefully*. It is difficult, but crucial, to be vulnerable.

The Sufis have a notion that experience and devotion will lead to "polishing the heart into a mirror." This is another name for the transformative education of being vulnerable, which no one can escape, though we can stall or distract ourselves from all that matters.

Let me tell you about three ways of being vulnerable. The first involves a quiet man whose life-changing moment is inspiring. He was Wu Feng, a Manchurian diplomat of the 1700s posted with an aboriginal tribe in the outskirts of Taiwan. Wu Feng befriended the aboriginal chief, whose tribe beheaded one of its members every year as a form of sacrifice.

Each year Wu Feng pleaded with all of his compassion and reverence for life that the chief put an end to this custom. The chief would listen respectfully as Wu Feng would plead, and then, after listening and bowing, the chief would summon the chosen tribe member and, without hesitation, behead him.

Finally, after living with the tribe for twenty-five years, Wu Feng once more pleaded with the chief to stop this senseless killing. But this time, when the tribe member was called forth, Wu Feng took his place and said, "No, if you will kill this time, it will be me."

The chief stared long into his friend's eyes, and having grown to love Wu Feng, he could not kill him. From that day, the practice of beheading stopped.

Of course, Wu Feng could have been killed, but his courage shows us that, at a certain point, how we live inside takes priority. At a certain point for each of us, talk evaporates and words cannot bring love into the open. In the end, it is not enough to *think* what we know. We must *live* it. Only by living it can love show itself as the greatest principle.

There are many questions and lessons waiting in this story. Key to them all is: What made Wu Feng finally put himself in the middle of the issue? What made watching become intolerable?

What ounce of inner courage, starting in what quiet corner of Wu Feng's soul, moved him to stand before the chief? And what ounce of courage finally opened the chief to change? Where does the Wu Feng in us live? Where the chief? How do we make a practice of moving, like Wu Feng, from watching to standing by our core? And how do we, like the chief, make a practice of softening our adherence to a tradition or old pattern that kills, and so open ourselves to love?

The second story comes from our own time. Richard Luttrell is a Vietnam vet, a gentle soul from the Midwest who thirty-nine years ago found himself as a young man in the jungles of Southeast Asia. Quickly, he fell into hand-to-hand combat with another young man. They didn't speak the same language though they faced the same terror. Richard wound up killing his counterpart. It was his first kill. As his fellow soldiers were looting the body, Richard pulled a small photograph from the dead man's wallet. It was of the young man and his little girl. "I remember holding the photo and actually squatting and getting close and actually looking in his face and looking at the photo and looking in his face."

The quiet American soldier kept the photo. Through the years, it called to him and plagued him. He became obsessed with it, as it kept the humanity of the man he had killed alive in his heart. Finally, it depressed him. He tried to get rid of it. When the Vietnam Memorial was built in Washington, D.C., Richard made a pilgrimage and left the small, unlabeled picture at the wall. But it was gathered into a book called *Offerings from the Wall*, and through a fellow vet, it made its way back to him.

So the improbable journey continued, wherein Richard Luttrell found the little girl in the snapshot. She is Lan Trong Ngoan, the daughter of the man he killed so many years ago. Compelled by a yearning to give the photo back, Richard and his wife flew to Vietnam, where he gave the small photo to this forty-year-old woman, who had no picture of her father.

Through an interpreter, Richard introduced himself. "Tell her this is the photo I took from her father's wallet the day I shot and killed him and that I'm returning it." With a cracking voice, he then asked for her forgiveness. After an awkward moment, Lan burst into tears and fell into his arms, and there, the two held each other up against our century, sobbing and embracing.

We have so much to learn from Richard Luttrell and Lan Trong Ngoan. What sort of quiet courage kept Richard's heart open, for all those years, to the pain of what he'd done? What made him listen to that pain and not seal it over? What enabled him to surrender to some journey he couldn't understand? What led him with Gandhi-like love to seek out Lan and return to Vietnam? And what made Lan want to meet him? What gave her the courage to forgive him? To fall into the arms of the man who killed her father? Like the immense example of South Africa, how do we find the inner steps that allow us to knit our wounds together, so we might put down our allegiances to those wounds like rusty weapons?

The third story comes from my good friend George. He just returned from Bali. Still jet-lagged, his eyes are incredibly clear. And the image he's carried back, the one he is eager to speak of, is of Hindu women flowing in their sarongs, wearing wide-brimmed hats filled with small bowls woven of palm and banana leaves. Each bowl is filled with a handful of rice and topped with a few petals. Every day, they deliver these throughout the village. One by one, they cup each bowl into place, into every opening they can find, as an offering to the gods that everyone feels but which no one can see. Every day, these kind people leave their little offerings in doorways, in stairwells, on roads, on windowsills, on the black sand that rims the sea. They place the tiny woven bowls so carefully that even the gods have to bow to inhale the gift.

George and I talk about this for quite some time. He is struck by the way these simple quiet people aren't *saying* they are grateful but are *being* grateful and how these gestures soften the climate. It makes me wonder, what if we teach the children how to bless every opening, how to bow to every threshold? What if we slip it in between when they learn how to tie their shoes and how to count? In a generation's time, would our fear of each other quiet down? Would we celebrate the unexpected? What if we were to place such a small bowl at each other's feet? What if we were to treat each other as openings to be blessed every day?

It seems the act of blessing is a lesson we have to earn, and for this reason it is not really hidden but allowed by grace to grow where it is still difficult for us to spoil. And so, somewhere in the midst of four hundred islands that we call Indonesia, thirteen time zones away, on a small island of black sand, in the north away from the thirsty tourists, the elegant women of Bali quietly place the small bowls of rice and flowers at your door before you wake to bless the opening we call the day. Such a simple secret, one that God has tucked away till we are vulnerable enough to find it.

The Beauty of It

If all I have is Now, where will I look for Joy? Without hope for
the future, without hope that things will change, with no hope
of finding what's been lost, and no hope of restoring the past,
with only the risk to crack open all that has hardened about me,
what will I do with what I have?

Our task in living is how, not why. When we suffer, we get
thrown into why: Why me? Why you? Why at this time? At best,
why distracts us. At worst, it stalls us. What we do know is that
life can be both miraculous and harsh, tender and devastating. At
times, we need to feel everything to make it through. At other
times, we need to empty ourselves in order not to drown in our
pain. When the surge of pain, or confusion, or awe is too great,
we shut down automatically—like a circuit breaker. This inner
reflex protects us from too potent a dose of life. Most of the time
we can reset ourselves. Sometimes we can't.

In the mid-eighties, Asian women began to show up at clin-
ics in and around Los Angeles complaining of sudden blindness. When tested, nothing physiological was found wrong with
their eyes. They were thought to be faking in order to receive
disability benefits. These isolated cases grew in number until a
subpopulation was recognized, all suffering the same inexplicable blindness. Finally, it was discovered that these women had
migrated from Cambodia, where they had witnessed unspeak-

able horrors, often perpetrated on their loved ones. In fact, they were all suffering from a traumatic blindness, their own form of post-traumatic stress. Even the trip across the Pacific couldn't stop the terrible scenes from replaying or stop the fear that new unspeakable horrors would keep surprising them. At some point, their spirit mercifully shut down their sight in order to protect the tender center of their being.

Of course, the horrors were now inside their eyes, so it's unclear if this sudden blindness protected them at all. But their plight has stayed with me as an example that, even within the art of facing things, there is a time not to look. And yet, in the deeper logic of our suffering, this is not inconsistent with the vow to remember such atrocities as Cambodia or the Holocaust. Sometimes we need to look away so that we can heal enough to tell the story.

In my own small version of this, I travel great distances to speak of my journey through cancer and what it's done to me. Yet I must swallow hard and look away every time a needle is poked in my vein. From outside, these things seem like contradictions—this looking and not looking, this search for truth only to shut down in the face of too difficult an experience. From inside, we are drawn into resilience through paradox. The poet Stanley Kunitz speaks to the urgent beauty of it all when he declares that "[t]he deepest thing I know is that I am living and dying at once, and my conviction is to report that self-dialogue." This kind of honest livelihood requires *both* feeling and emptying in the same way that breathing requires inhaling and exhaling. There is no way around it.

Feeling and Emptying

O leaf that grows
in full sun, teach us
how to receive
what touches us,
letting the rest
spill off.

On the one hand, being free of heart depends on our ability to engage all our feelings. For living *in* this messy, disorderly flood of relationship that we call life is how we discover that we are subject to the same currents. And accepting that we are in the same roar of currents is the source of compassion. Without such compassion, we are always a veil away from feeling life directly. On the other hand, being free of mind requires letting go in a way that keeps emptying us of the residue of our experience. Otherwise, when allowed to build, that residue can block the immediacy of our perception. Without such emptying, we are also a veil away from feeling life directly.

The Musqueam tribe of the First Nations of Canada has an ethic called *sqwallowing*, which is *the art of bringing the heart and mind together.* Central to this native art is the tending of all human moods. Such a commitment comes from a belief that regarding our human moods together unfetters the flow of Spirit. To access Spirit then, we need to accept all of our emotions—that is, we need to let them touch us and move on through. It is this thoroughness (feeling) and throughness (emptying) that opens us to the Source.

The leading religious scholar Lawrence Sullivan speaks to the art of feeling and emptying as our chance to cultivate a wholeness of heart. He captures this paradox beautifully when he suggests that our fullness is tied to our emptiness in the way that the chamber of an instrument, such as a guitar or a cello, is only resonant when its hollow center is clear and unobstructed. This is true because when clear and unobstructed, there is room for the music to fill itself out and emerge. Likewise, only when our heart is clear and unobstructed can we reverberate with the music of being alive. This is profound. Nevertheless, this is difficult to discern and live into, for we often resist both feeling what comes our way and being empty.

In his 1961 film *Through a Glass Darkly*, the great Swedish filmmaker Ingmar Bergman offers a compelling example of how we all resist both feeling and emptying. In the film, David, a novelist too circumscribed by his art, confesses to his troubled daughter, "One draws a magic circle around oneself to keep everything out that does not fit one's secret games. Each time life breaks through the circle, the games become puny and ridiculous. So one draws a new circle and builds new defenses . . . [Then life breaks through again and, if fortunate, we] are forced to live in reality."

David, like many of us, has become skilled in the wrong art: *maneuvering around life* rather than *living our way through*. So what does your magic circle look like? What aspects of your boundaries are unnecessary? Are you aware of your secret games? One of my early secret games was to hide within the magic circle of my poetry, watching life but seldom letting life touch me. A later secret game was the attempt to make myself invaluable to those I loved, in hopes that they would feel indebted to love me back. Eventually, I was broken and humbled to accept living in the world, outside of my magic circle. I was forced by both wonder and pain to risk life beyond my defenses, where, yes, I was often hurt, but where I was profoundly touched by life. Inexplicable as it is, leaning into life in this way makes pain bearable.

So let's explore the art of feeling (inhaling our experience) and emptying (exhaling our experience), which when leaned into can help us live. I have no clear picture of how this all works, only a handful of learnings. Here are four.

—— :: ——

1. *Letting what-is lead the way.* Like the sun, the hard beauty of life is so dazzling that, though we seek it directly, we can seldom look at it squarely. And so we often glimpse the heat of life and glance away into the past or the future. But the threshold to meaning is in *accepting what-is*, not looking back through *should have* and not looking forward through *what if.* The present is a fiery lover, difficult to live with but impossible to live without. But worse is the draining seduction to relive the past or defer our life into an imagined future. Though often hypnotic, neither allows us to feel or empty. They simply preoccupy us. Reliving and deferring keep us from the task of living.

2. *Expressing what remains unexpressed.* This keeps the heart and mind transparent and hollow. Like exercise that keeps the body flush and possible, expression allows for experience to flow directly. It allows what we encounter to actually reach inside and touch us, not just mix with the unprocessed silt that has built up around our heart. We all know the times that there is nothing in the way and how clean that feels. And we all know the feeling of being stuck and numb when something painful lodges behind the heart or eye. But how do we clear ourselves? How do we loosen what is stuck and

keep life streaming through? I only know that when feeling stuck, I can express what it feels like to be so stuck, and something loosens. And when feeling numb, I can express the last meaningful feelings I had, and something begins to flow on through.

3. *Acknowledging and forgiving our unconscious participation in life.* Each of us, no matter how aware, kind, or diligent, will participate in unconscious living. This means that, at one time or another, we all act in ways that are self-centered and inconsiderate or hurtful. Inadvertently, we will act out some need to be loved or accepted, or replay some script we don't even know we are replaying, passing on our wound. So we all hurt others, often through our unconscious acts. It goes with the territory of being human. It's what learning and forgiving are all about: how to transform and reform ourselves by understanding what we've done or not done, and how to make amends. This acknowledgment and forgiveness helps us to see and accept our humanness with accuracy and compassion. The more we can accept and forgive our own unconscious life (past and present), the greater our compassion for the humanness of others. The more conscious and transparent our hearts and minds, the more compassionate a community we will find ourselves creating.

4. *Keeping our mind-heart open.* Once unclogged of unexpressed feelings, and once at home in our humanness, we have more of a chance to experience fully whatever comes our way — lessening the degree to which we distort new experience by denying or massaging our very human flaws. The challenge is to accept the fact and truth of each feeling as it comes through, neither beating it off nor holding onto it.

— :: —

These dynamics of heart may appear in our lives in sequence, but they often overlap. However they appear, they keep doing so in ongoing cycles, as the life of experience doesn't end. And just as we keep our cars running smoothly, we must keep our hearts running smoothly. Just as we must change the oil, put air in our tires, and clean our windshield continually, we must regularly express what builds up within us, acknowledge and forgive our unconscious participation in life, and keep our cleansed heart open.

Diving Down and Coming Up

I had a great teacher in all of this, though I spent very little time with him. He was the poet I quoted earlier, the remarkable Stanley Kunitz, who died recently at the age of 100. Others knew him better and studied with him longer. Through his work, it was clear that the longer he lived, the more he became a holy poem himself. He once defined art as the "chalice into which we pour the wine of transcendence."

I remember a time, almost twenty-five years ago, when he came to the University of Albany, where I taught. He read in a hall to about three hundred of us, his soft rhythmic voice boring below our masks, giving rise to the one place we all swim in. When he finished, a young student raised his hand and asked, "How long did it take to write that poem?"

I will never forget how he started to answer, and then, as if distracted by the voice of an angel that only he could hear, he peered off above us for what seemed like minutes of silence. He returned to the crowd and answered, "My whole life."

With that, he made me realize that as we only see a dolphin when it breaks surface, because it spends most of its life out of view in the deep, so it is with the poet and the artist and the lover aching to be loved. Stanley was such a dolphin breaking surface before us that night. His confessing as much affirmed the truth that we are all poets and artists and lovers. He made me realize that even when silent in the deep, we are writing poems and birthing art and loving. And more importantly, the poem is writing itself before breaking surface through us, as the love is writing itself into the world. The beauty of it all is that though the gesture of life breaking surface like a dolphin stuns us, none of this—not the poem, the painting, the music, or the act of courage or love—is possible without the labor that takes place out of sight in the deep.

So let's stop making these useless distinctions between what we see and what we don't, between what we know and what we don't, between what is silent and what is said, even between being and doing. Let's even stop pretending that breaking surface is what it is all for, magnificent as that is. We are born to thread our lives between depth and surface without end, feeling and emptying as we go, with no finished arrival in mind. Down there, living and poetry are one, and love and courage and frailty are one. In truth, everything that matters grows out of view in the deep. The beauty is that the diving down and coming up—never sure where we will break surface next—is the art of living, and we are the ever-changing work of art.

A Myth of Encouragement

We run the length of our cage and rattle our dreams.
Never seeing that the bars are wide enough
to slip through.

While working on understanding what it means to give up what
no longer works, I had a conversation with my wife Susan and
my dear friend and mentor Joel. That night I had a dream.

Joel was my father, and the three of us were roping down our
sailboat in preparation for a hurricane. The water began to rise
around the rails. But something else was more threatening. Joel
had stood up to area thugs on principle, holding his ground about
something, and we were anticipating a reprisal. He had finished
tying down the bow and went inside. Susan and I were finishing
up when two hooded men, one large, the other small, appeared
out of the bushes with hammers. They jumped on the boat and
began hammering the hull beneath the waterline. I tried to stop
them, but the larger man threatened to hit me with his hammer.
Somehow, I wrestled the hammer from the smaller one, pinned
him beneath me, and threatened to hit him in the head, if the
larger one didn't stop. At this, the larger man removed his hood
and dropped his hammer, which Susan picked up. We ordered
them off the boat and brought them into the house.

The tall one was blond and burly. When I removed the hood
from the smaller one, I discovered he was just a boy, no more

than ten. The way their eyes flashed between them, I knew they were father and son. As we sat there, Joel returned, assessed the situation immediately, put his hand on the tall one's shoulder, and said, "You must be cold. Would you like some tea?"

Startled, the larger thug nodded yes. Joel motioned for me to let the smaller one up. He ran to his father. Joel brought them tea and cocoa, then sat beside the larger thug and simply asked, "Why?"

The large blond man dropped his shoulders, "I'm sorry. I don't do this sort of thing. I'm a social studies teacher, eighth grade . . ." He paused to sip his tea, very embarrassed, "I was laid off and my wife is sick . . . I agreed to break up your boat, but I never would have hurt you . . . or anyone."

We all stared at each other. The hull of the boat was slowly taking water where he had hammered through. The large man put his face in his hands, "My boy doesn't have any toys . . ."

This alarmed Joel, who took the large man's hammer from Susan, rushed to his father's wooden desk, which he had brought with him from Europe, and began hammering the top in an ef-fort to free something. I went to stop him, but he waved me off. The desk was too strong to break. He finally threw the hammer down, removed the top drawer, turned it over, and gave it to the boy as a toy house.

The boy began to glow. Susan gave him pencils and paper clips, and the little one smiled. He became a boy again and began to play, imagining the clips and pencils were us. And he danced us around in his new play house till we all sat at a make-believe table, having dinner. He made up our conversation and began to laugh for each of us. We sat in silence, watching the little boy play. Our boat was slightly underwater by now.

Something came across Joel's eyes and he took the teacup from the blond father and said, "Go. I will say that you have done what you were asked. Go take care of your wife . . . and take the toy for the boy."

The stunned blond father hugged Joel, and we all hugged each other and sent those who came to harm us back into the night.

What Is Necessary

I want to learn more and more to see as beautiful what is
necessary . . . then I shall be one of those who makes
things beautiful.
❖ *Friedrich Wilhelm Nietzsche*

Friedrich Wilhelm Nietzsche (1844–1900) was a German philosopher who was largely overlooked during his short working
life. Nietzsche is well-known today for his searing look at the in-
exorable forces of life. He is often used by the willful to reinforce
and even deify their belief in individual will as the most important force in meeting life. But Nietzsche himself is a remarkable
story of transformation that is seldom talked about. In his own
thinking, he stopped talking about the *will to power* and began
to explore a *love of fate*. Over time, he found his mental frame
undone as he was reshaped from a belief that we control our
own destiny to accepting that we are part of what he called an
eternal recurrence. He put down his belief in self-preservation at all
cost in favor of seeing what is necessary as beautiful. Ultimately,
life turned Nietzsche inside out, breaking the shell of a nay-sayer
to reveal the softer center of a yes-sayer. Those who build their
case in the world on Nietzsche's early understandings of will see
this transformation as a fall, as an unfortunate breakdown of his
steely clarity. I see it as the beautiful and archetypal unfolding of
the tender flower that is the soul.

Upon his death, Nietzsche's sister compiled a book from his extensive journals. She called it *The Will to Power*, after her brother's early thinking. In those journals, Nietzsche declares that living things are not just driven by the mere need to stay alive, but by a greater need to wield and use power, to dominate others, and to make them weaker:

A living thing seeks above all to discharge its strength—life itself is will to power; self-preservation is only one of the indirect and most frequent results. Every specific body strives to become master over all space and to extend its force [its will to power] and to thrust back all that resists its extension.

Not a pretty picture. Take a tablespoon of Nietzsche and a tablespoon of Darwin, add boiling water, and you have a dark aggressive world in which the stronger and more intelligent hoard and burn every resource they can find, including each other. At its worst, this promotes a moral cannibalism. Obviously, I do not cotton to this worldview. Nonetheless, Nietzsche describes an aspect of the human enterprise that has shown its ugly head throughout history. When self-centeredness, no matter how dressed, is served above all else, the will to power becomes a god. This is not inevitable but a path we choose.

Perhaps the most widely quoted phrase of Nietzsche is "God is dead." But like so many utterances across time, it is often quoted out of context. The full quote follows:

God is dead. God remains dead. And we have killed him. How shall we, murderers of all murderers, console ourselves? Who will wipe this blood off us? With what water could we purify ourselves? What

festivals of atonement, what sacred games shall we need to invent? Is
not the greatness of this deed too great for us? Must we not ourselves
become gods simply to be worthy of it?

More than pronouncing that God is dead, Nietzsche seems to
be lamenting that we have murdered His possibility. And in his
lament he crystallizes the plight we have wrought for ourselves
(to install ourselves as gods) and the solution we avoid (the sacred games we need to invent to restore our humility and compassion). It's no different in the tumble of a single life when we,
in our arrogance and skepticism, murder wonder and awe. The
need to believe in and rely on something larger than us doesn't
go away.

In his own turmoil, Nietzsche found this to be true. He finally
answers his constant question (What makes liberation possible?)
by stating, "No longer being ashamed in front of oneself." The
will to power and the constant fight against the world peels back,
at last, to the simple act of being who we are in front of ourselves
and the world. For all of his outward persistence in standing up
to a relentless world, he, like so many sages and humbled war-
riors before him, is undone by the simple need to be—to feel
the rain on his face and the night in his heart—without muf-
fling either the cries of the living or the breath of Spirit that
keeps us going.

Now liberation depends on unstrapping our armor, not on
thickening it. Now courage depends on feeling the immense
fragility of the simplest living thing, without minimizing either
its magnificence or its terrible chance of being snuffed. It is this
turn of revelation that leads Nietzsche to blueprint his notion of
eternal recurrence. Here, he posits that time runs its course and

then repeats exactly and infinitely. And so the absurdities and pains of life must be endured not only once, but repeatedly and forever. With a new sense of humility, Nietzsche now imagines that the nihilist would find such a Universe torturous, but for one who has learned to be a yes-sayer, such an existence could be bliss.

It is from this plateau on his climb through life that Nietzsche finally writes:

I want to learn more and more to see as beautiful what is necessary . . . then I shall be one of those who makes things beautiful. Amor fati *(love of fate): let that be my love henceforth! I do not want to wage war against what is ugly. I do not want to accuse; I do not even want to accuse those who accuse.* Looking away *shall be my only negation. And all in all and on the whole: some day I wish to be only a* Yes-sayer.

Less than two years after writing this, Nietzsche suffered a mental collapse. He was forty-four. No one will ever know exactly what happened. Like Van Gogh, and almost at the same time, Nietzsche's sensibilities seem to have heightened. Having spent so much of his life removing the thinking of others from impeding his direct experience of life, and continuing courageously to remove his own thinking as well, it appears he was brought burningly close to the raw pulse of life.

The story goes that, on January 3, 1889, he was approached by two policemen after making some sort of public disturbance in the streets of Turin. It seems he saw a horse being whipped at the other end of the Piazza Carlo Alberto, and so ran to the horse, throwing his arms around its neck to protect it. Then he collapsed to the ground. He never recovered. Some regard this event as embarrassing and others discount its veracity, and yet it just might be Nietzsche's crowning moment of integrity on par with St. Francis of Assisi displaying his unmitigated love for all of God's creatures.

I find it beautiful and heartbreaking that all the vast and tenacious thinking of such a prodigious mind should undo itself—quite naturally and poignantly, indeed, quite inevitably—into the compassionate act of protecting a horse from being whipped. In that moment, standing between the whip and the whipped becomes necessary. When we can say yes and throw our arms around the beast's neck, then what feels morally required stuns us with its splendor.

Like Job moaning stubbornly to God in his endless arias of why, like Jacob wrestling the unnamed angel in the ravine, like Keats collapsing into the truth and beauty before him, Nietzsche wrestled the tensions of suffering into what it means to be alive. Finally, he seems to have settled on the need to bravely and starkly part the veil of knowledge behind which life, in its beautiful and unbearable rawness, waits to reduce us to what is essential. In that naked humility, we can accept life on its own terms and be transformed. This naked embrace is the difference between murdering the possibility of God and participating in God, between thick pessimism and transparent optimism.

The fear of endless breakdown is what saddens our dark side to see life as one long collapse, while a belief in transformation empowers our humbler side to see life as one endless shaping of all that is living into a unity that keeps the world going. This tension between breakdown and transformation seems to have marked the unfolding of Nietzsche's mind from his early notion of will to power to his earned notion of love of fate.

In truth, a heart-door swings between a world of breakdown in which we scramble against each other to survive and a world of transformation in which we are worn of what is extraneous until we fit together in a beautiful harmony that preserves life. The hinge of that heart-door is the courage to face and accept life directly and completely on its own terms. Until, as Nietzsche finally utters, what is necessary becomes beautiful.

Humility and Awe

Sometimes, the weight of things
brings us to our knees, and we
are forced to see the underside,
and there, the light of God
is awash, breaking all
principle.

At once, there is nothing new and yet no one has ever lived
what you are about to live. This is a timeless paradox that we
frequently fall to either side of. Accepting one without the other
can suppress or seduce us into a false, imbalanced life. When we
accept that *nothing is new* as our primary truth, we can slip into
a state of insignificance that is defeating: *What do I matter? What
does anything matter?* Yet the other side alone is just as dangerous.
When we accept that *everything is possible and dependent on our
actions* as our primary truth, we can puff up into a state of grandiosity: *I can change the world; everything depends on what I do.*

But just as we need two eyes in order to perceive depth, we
need both aspects of this paradox in order to perceive the depth
of the Universe. For the fact that nothing is new quiets our conquering will back into humility. And the fact that everything is
possible lifts our defeated insignificance into awe. Together, humility and awe enable us to face the raw power of life that is

always present and at work behind our one-sided commitments to surviving and escaping pain.

So when feeling insignificant as a bug or like a pharaoh in search of your pyramid, it helps to remember that sunrise is the act of turning toward a light that is always there. The sun doesn't rise for us. We turn to it and the day begins. Likewise, when we stop pretending that things rise before us, the truth and majesty of things reveal themselves. Then, through humility and awe, facing and bowing become the same act of praise.

Beginning Again

If the angel deigns to come, it will be because you have convinced her, not by tears but by your humble resolve to be always beginning; to be a beginner.

❖ *Rainer Maria Rilke*

So here we are, after another curious journey through the sweet labyrinth we call being alive. Always, after so many stories and questions, there is little to say and more to know. As if truth will only break down to another beginning. I guess that is the point. We are left with this unimpeachable process by which we unfold back into innocence. Always beginning, as Rilke says. Because only in beginning is life incredibly close. This does not mean we should coldly jettison the past. That a butterfly appears does not make its cocoon false. That we grow does not make who we were untrue. Each self is necessary and real.

I confess I have returned to the sea many times to hear my purpose again. And I have returned to love, a sea whose storms have almost drowned me, because I swear it's not the sea that causes the storm. When all is said and done or left undone, I need the sea, the love, the journey back to innocence. And failing to find them, I must wait till I am broken, till my stubbornness is cracked, till I am forced to start over, not knowing what I want or need.

In truth, I keep looking for one more teacher, only to find that fish learn from the water and birds learn from the sky. So if you want to learn about the sea, it helps to be at sea. If you want to learn about compassion, it helps to be in love. If you want to learn about healing, it helps to know of suffering. The strong live in the storm without worshipping the storm. This is what it means to stay in conversation with life.

You see, somewhere along the way, I realized that all the separate conversations are part of one conversation, and all the different questions are part of one inquiry, and all the colorful beings who ask, suffer, talk, and listen are part of one common element of being that binds us in the human family. And that element is precious and resilient. It can save our lives. I now accept that only by staying in this conversation together can we find the love and truth that helps us live. Without each other, we miss much of what we know. Without the courage to face each other and hold each other, we remain broken and adrift. It seems simple, but staying in conversation in this way is a source of joy. Our job is to nourish the spark of life we each carry inside.

I admit that I am still listening for what courage has to say. I am still enduring the holes being carved in the flute of my soul, still wrestling with the unnamed angel at the bottom of my ravine.

If asked, I must say that life has become a climb up an endless mountain where I have been surprised more than once by the howl of a wolf that no one can see. It makes God's depth audible. Now I realize that all the cries I've heard to the bone have done the same. And tiring on the way, I've been soothed by the vastness and the scent of flowers blossoming out of view. It's made me grateful that each of us carries a flower waiting to bloom behind our eyes—a flower that some have called the soul.

This conversation—between the crying of the wolf and the scent of the flower, between the cries heard to the bone and the blossoming of the soul—has occupied much of my life. It's where I hear what I call truth. It's where I settle, often exhausted, into what I know as love. It is the wilderness I am drawn to, which always compels me back into the thick tangle of the living.

Again, I lift my head from my troubles, my heart suddenly open to the sky reflected in your eyes. Again, I have wonderfully come to the edge of all I know, to the edge of even knowing what to ask. What opens here? What remains real? What is worth holding on to, when more arises from letting go? The longer I live—the longer I lean into living—the deeper I know myself and the well from which we all spring. This makes it harder to say what it means to have a personal identity, which, when facing death, drops away like a familiar robe. It seems deeper forms of nakedness are required the closer we get to what matters. Yet only in such raw moments do I feel most truly myself.

Like monks whose daily charge is to sweep leaves from the path—though, even as they sweep, more leaves cover the path—it is our daily charge to uncover our innocence and trust and Beginner's Mind, so that we may renew our closeness to what is sacred.

So what shall we talk about next? What shall we look at in silence together? To talk means, more and more, to listen. And to listen means, more and more, to be undone by awe or pain in each other's presence. Who's to say this isn't what elephants remember when sleeping under the stars or what fish do when they chase light together? That we grow simpler by accepting what we experience is a precious bit of wisdom—more smelling salt than gem. So let's keep ourselves awake by splashing love on each other's face. When we can get out of the way, it's what we do best. It's what we are put here for.

Gratitudes

To my dear friends. Whenever we meet, it isn't long before we peer somewhere between us; fishing for those images of love and truth that flash close to the surface before turning back into the deep. All we seem to do now is travel great distances to find each other, or those like us, in order to ask the simplest of questions.

Especially Eileen, Bob, Jill, Dave, Pat, Steve, Karen, Paul, Pam, George, Paula, Pam, Skip, Don, TC, Charles, Ellen, Eleanor, and Joel and Sally. Gratitude as well to Loretta Barrett for your wisdom and steadfast belief in art that matters. And to Jan Johnson, Caroline Pincus, and Brenda Knight at Red Wheel/Weiser for your care and excellence.

A special bow to Wayne Muller for your welcome to everyone and everything, and to Parker Palmer for your fierce love of all that is essential, and to Paul Bowler for your companionship and for our thirty-year conversation. To Robert Mason for holding the washcloth to my head more than once. And to my wife, Susan, for always leading with your heart.

And gratitude to those I've journeyed with in workshops around the country. For the wisdom of so many people who in a quiet, unexpected circle of truth shared their stories. And to my readers. Having readers at all is a gift no writer can ever assume. That so many of you have been kind enough to share the questions and lessons of your lives is something for which I am very grateful. You have all taught me much about courage. I feel like a weed allowed to root in the most beautiful garden. Thank you all.

Notes

Epigraph

"If your everyday practice is to open to all your emotions . . ." From Pema Chödrön, *Start Where You Are: A Guide to Compassionate Living* (Boston: Shambhala, 1994).

Movement I: Facing The Lion
Wings of the Butterfly

p. 16, line 2: "Her story took place in Guatemala . . ." In a letter, Kathleen Kostelny, a courageous woman who travels the world working with children of war, told me the story of this little Guatemalan girl, Flor, "who suffered her parents being killed by soldiers. One day, when the sun moved down the mountain, she ran to the fields to greet her parents. Her mother would often scold her for running so fast, and her father would scoop her up in his strong arms. But now, her mother and father lay on the soft brown earth. 'Levante! Levante!' Get up! Get up!' she demanded. They did not move, even when she began to cry.

"When her brother came back from market, he held her to his chest and rocked her all night, murmuring, 'Pobrecita, Pobrecita' until the sun came up. The next day they buried their parents in the fields of corn under the Bilboa tree. That night her brother told her that he was going away to be a soldier.

"Three years passed since the soldiers came to her finca in the mountains, and since her brother went away. The sun danced on Flor's fingers as she gently cradled a butterfly of vivid blues and purples in her tiny brown hands. 'Pobrecita,' poor little one, she laughed, taking the creature between her small fingers, then pausing briefly before ripping the trembling wing from its body and letting it drop to the soft earth.

"The butterfly struggled to free itself with its remaining wing, even as the little fingers peeled it slowly from its body. She dropped the lifeless remains. Then, with her bare foot, crushed the useless body in the soft Guatemalan dirt."

p. 17, line 5: " . . . rather than face the undiscovered country in himself . . ." From *Gilgamesh, A Verse Narrative*, translated by Herbert Mason (New York: New American Library, 1972), p. 27. This exceptional translation is rendered in language so close to the heart that it is both ancient and immediate.

p. 18, line 5: "Let us present the same face to everyone . . ." From *Hua Hu Ching: The Unknown Teachings of Lao Tzu*, translated by Brian Walker (San Francisco: HarperSanFrancisco, 1992).

p. 19, line 8: "He had not come to terms with his own brokenness . . ." From Jean Vanier, *Becoming Human* (Mahway, NJ: Paulist Press, 1998).

Vengeance or Music

p. 20, epigraph: "When pushed below . . ." Unless otherwise noted, the epigraphs throughout are written by the author.

p. 20, line 8: "Years later, I learned . . ." From Gerald May, "The Vengeance Reflex," *Shalem News*, Fall 2001.

p. 21, line 11: "The movie isn't about Hitler's great crimes . . ." Menno Meyjes quoted in Jamie Melanowski's "Human, Yes, But No Less a Monster," *New York Times*, December 22, 2002, pp. 1, 36.

Wrestling with God

p. 24, line 17: ". . . the Old Testament story of Jacob . . ."
From James Frazer, *Folklore in the Old Testament* (New York: Avenel Books, 1988), pp. 251–52.

p. 28, line 2: "Lao Tzu says, having without possessing . . ."
From *Tao Teh Ching*, translated by Stephen Mitchell (New York: Harper & Row, 1988), p. 10.

p. 28, line 23: ". . . this poem by a fourth grader . . ."
John Rybicki is a poet and teacher in Kalamazoo, Michigan. He teaches writing and creative expression to elementary students in the city of Detroit. After the tragedy of 9/11, he had them write short poems, giving them the first line: *If you are lucky in this life . . .* Several of the poems, including this one, were collected and published in *North American Review.*

The Boy and the Drum

p. 32, line 1: "There is an old Hindu story . . ." From *Tell These Secrets: Tales of Generosity from Around the World*, unpublished manuscript. An amazing collection of seventy-four stories gathered from twenty-three traditions and edited by Ian Simmons and Margo McLoughlin. Many of the stories are available as a teaching resource at *www.LearningtoGive.org/materials/folktales.* This story of the boy and the drum was originally collected by A. K. Ramanujan in his *Folktales from India: A Selection of Oral Tales from Twenty-two Languages* (New York: Pantheon Books, 1991). There, he speaks of this story as one that shaped him as a boy.

The Swan and the Tailor

p. 38, line 17: "A tailor by trade, Woolman lived . . ."
From Parker J. Palmer, "The Politics of the Broken-Hearted: On

Holding the Tensions of Democracy," in *Deepening the American Dream: Reflections on the Inner Life and Spirit of Democracy*, edited by Mark Nepo (San Francisco: Jossey-Bass, 2005), p. 360. In this essay and further in his remarks as a keynote speaker at the National Press Club in Washington, D.C., at a Fetzer Institute–sponsored conference held on September 27, 2005, Palmer offers profound insights regarding the courage it takes to live in the tensions of unanswered conflicts, not acting prematurely, but staying in relationship despite our differences.

Living within Patterns

p. 50, line 6: "When my dear friend Wayne was staying in Peru . . ." In his essential book *How Then Shall We Live* (New York: Bantam, 1999), Wayne Muller speaks of his journey to the small pueblo of Yanque in the mountains of south central Peru (pp. 137–39) and how he later experienced the importance of clearing the acequia, again, among the people of Truchas, in northern New Mexico (pp. 73–76).

Facing Ourselves

p. 64, epigraph: "Consciously or unconsciously . . ." From J. Krishnamurti, *The First and Last Freedom* (San Francisco: HarperSanFrancisco, 1954), p. 281.

p. 65, line 29: "In his compelling and mysterious apprenticeship with the sorcerer Don Juan . . ." As a young anthropology student, Carlos Castenada encountered the sorcerer Don Juan and became a reluctant apprentice. His journey and learnings from the Yaqui shaman can be found in a series of books. For a comprehensive sense of Don Juan's teachings, though, I refer you to the magical *Journey to Ixtlan*.

p. 67, line 4: "Any life, no matter how long . . ." From the journal *The Sun* (July 2005, Issue 355), p. 48.

The Life of the Lion

p. 68, line 8: "Nearly all cultures have stories of the lion which represent the best and worst of what it means to be human." For another contemporary investigation of the life of the lion, please see Jane Hirshfield's essay "Facing the Lion: The Way of Shadow and Light in Some Twentieth Century Poems" in her penetrating book *Nine Gates: Entering the Mind of Poetry* (New York: HarperCollins, 1997), pp. 153–75. The entire book is a compelling guide to the way the mind of poetry awakens our fundamental sense of being.

p. 71, line 27: "Power properly understood . . ." From Martin Luther King, Jr., last presidential address to the Southern Christian Leadership Conference, 1967.

Facing Each Other

p. 74, epigraph: "Conveyed from mouth to ear . . ." From *Teachings of the Jewish Mystics,* edited by Perle Besserman (Boston: Shambhala, 1998), p. xi.

p. 76, line 3: "If the character of a person . . ." From James Hillman, *The Force of Character* (New York: Random House, 1999), pp. 185–86.

Sympathetic Fibers

p. 79, line 21: "If I recognize the interconnectedness . . ." From Claude Anshin Thomas, *At Hell's Gate* (Boston: Shambhala, 2004). Cited in *The Sun* (Oct. 2004, Issue 346), pp. 12–19.

p. 80, line 23: "Ubuntu is the essence of being human . . ." from a foreword by Desmond Tutu in *Exploring Forgiveness,* edited by Robert D. Enright and Joanna North (Madison, WI: University of Wisconsin Press, 1998).

p. 80, line 26: "Ubuntu is a Zulu word . . ." This definition is from Dirk J. Louw's paper, *Ubuntu: An African Assessment of the Religious Other,* presented at the twentieth World Congress of Philosophy in 1998. The paper is archived as part of the Paideia Project On-line, the online archive for the World Congress of Philosophy (*http://www.bu.edu/wcp/Papers/Afri/AfriLouw.htm*).

The Art of Encouragement

p. 89, line 24: "It is most surely true . . ." From Helen Luke, *Dark Wood to White Rose: The Journey of Transformation in Dante's Divine Comedy* (New York: Parabola, 1989), p. 11.

Standing by One's Core

p. 91, epigraph: "Solitude does not mean . . ." From Parker J. Palmer, *A Hidden Wholeness: The Journey Toward An Undivided Life* (San Francisco: Jossey-Bass, 2004), p. 55. This is from a remarkable chapter called "Being Alone Together."

p. 92, line 24: "The Aramaic word for heart, *lebak* . . ." From *Prayer of the Cosmos: Meditations on the Aramaic Words of Jesus,* translated by Neil Douglas-Klotz (San Francisco: HarperSanFrancisco, 1990), p. 81.

p. 95, line 6: "According to Erik Erikson . . ." From the introduction, by Robert N. Bellah, to *Deepening the American Dream: Reflections on the Inner Life and Spirit of Democracy,* edited by Mark Nepo (San Francisco: Jossey-Bass, 2005), p. vii.

The Heart of It

p. 98, line 10: "The cost of a thing . . ." Henry David Thoreau, as quoted in *The Sun* (June 2005, Issue 354), p. 48.

The Heart's Blossom

p. 106, epigraph: "It is the song from within . . ." From "Where the HeartBeast Sings," in my collected essays, *Unlearning Back to God: Essays on Inwardness, 1985–2005* (London, New York: Khaniqahi Nimatullahi Publications, 2006), p. 110.

p. 106, line 1: "All courage is threshold ⁻crossing . ‚‚⁻." This opening passage marks my first exploration into the topic of courage. It originally appeared as the July 1 entry in my spiritual daybook, *The Book of Awakening* (San Francisco: Red Wheel Weiser/Conari, 2000), p. 217.

p. 107, line 18: ". . . and asked that she be his teacher . . ." The woman who stopped Naropa was *Vajrayogini*, known as the Great Bliss Queen. Because his negative karma was not consciously faced, Naropa was only able to see her as a very ugly, old woman. His mental stains prevented him from seeing her true form. As a "wisdom-goddess," Vajrayogini cuts through an initiate's ignorance and severs them from their hindering attachments. Her name translates as the "space dancer of Naropa."

p. 108, line 20: "When I think of both More and Galileo . . ." Please see the outstanding plays *A Man For All Seasons* by Robert Bolt (1960) regarding Sir Thomas More and the oath, and *Galileo* by Bertolt Brecht (1940) about Galileo's struggle whether or not to recant.

p. 108, line 24: ". . . the great writer Aleksandr Solzhenitsyn . . ." After many years, Solzhenitsyn completed *The*

Gulag Archipelago, originally titled *The Soul and Barbed Wire*, a three-volume account exposing the Soviet prison system that included testimonies from 227 other prisoners. In 1970, he was awarded the Nobel Prize in Literature. In 1974, he was placed in exile from the Soviet Union.

A Sacred Becoming

p. 112, line 3: "For your soul . . ." From Kenneth Avery, "A Glimpse into 'Attar's Book of Mysteries," in *Sufi, A Journal of Sufism* (Spring 2005, Issue 65), pp. 43–44. This quote is from the *Asrar-nama (The Book of Mysteries)* by Shaykh Farid al-Din 'Attar (1142–1220). His other classic book is the *Mantiq al-Tayr (The Conference of the Birds)*.

Movement 2: Being the Lion

Fires Looking for a Sea

p. 115, line 9: "Some uncomprehended law . . ." From Florida Scott-Maxwell, *The Measure of My Days* (New York: Penguin Books, 1979).

Aliveness and Woundedness

p. 120, line 11: "Consider the *Chien* . . ." From *Mathews' Chinese-English Dictionary* (Cambridge, MA: Harvard University Press, 1960), p. 114.

Everything or Nothing

p. 124, line 3: "The chilling logic of depression . . ." From Don Raiche, "A Small Flame in Our Hands" (unpublished manuscript), p. 5.

p. 124, line 20: "Thus I suffered and was miserable . . ."
From C. G. Jung, "Letter to H. Kirsch," in *An Encyclopedia of Archetypal Symbolism* (Boston: Shambhala, 1997), pp. 416–17. Please see *Memories, Dreams, Reflections*, an inner autobiography dictated by Carl Jung at the age of eighty-one to one of his closest colleagues, Aniela Jaffé. It is a remarkable journey into the depths of one person's heart and what it means to be alive.

The Fall into Life
p. 128, line 24: "The sugar cane should welcome the cutting . . ." from the 1987 travel diary of Jeremy Waletzky.

p. 130, line 25: "a person's *adab* . . ." The contemporary Sufi scholar Qamar-ul Huda speaks to all this eloquently in an article called "Make Friends with One's Adab: Inner Meanings of Suhrawardi's Theology of Moral Conduct," in *Sufi, A Journal of Sufism* (Spring 2005, Issue 65), pp. 13–17. Qamar-ul Huda is author of *Striving for Divine Union: Spiritual Exercises for Suhrawardi Sufis* (New York: Routledge, 2003).

Four in the Morning
p. 132, line 11: ". . . the Dark Night of the Soul . . ." Please see Gerald May's *The Dark Night of the Soul* (San Francisco: HarperSanFrancisco, 2004) for a compelling and useful exploration of the connection between darkness and spiritual growth.

p. 133, line 14: "There are circumstances that must shatter you . . ." From Leon Wieseltier, *Kaddish* (New York: Vintage Books, 1998), p. 226.

p. 134, line 4: "To wear out one's intellect . . ." *Chuang Tzu: Mystic, Moralist and Social Reformer*, translated by Herbert A. Giles (London: Bernard Quaritch, 1989).

What Gets in the Way

**p. 140, epigraph: "Something we were withholding
. . ."** From "The Gift Outright" in *The Poetry of Robert Frost:
The Collected Poems, Complete and Unabridged*, edited by Edward
Connery Lathem (New York: Henry Holt & Co., 1969), p. 467.

p. 143, line 25: "alienation . . ." It was Emile Durkheim, a
French sociologist, who first introduced the concept of alienation
(*anomie*) in his book *The Division of Labor in Society*, published in
1893. He spoke about anomie as a way to describe a condition
of an ambiguous relationship that was occurring in his society.
This meant that values regarding how people should treat each
other were breaking down, and thus people didn't know what to
expect from one another. Durkheim proposed that as societies
become more complex, people are no longer tied to one another,
and social bonds become impersonal. Durkheim observed that
periods of drastic social disruption bring about greater anomie
and higher rates of crime, suicide, and deviance. He coined the
term as a type of suicide associated with the loss of a more rela-
tional way of life.

p. 144, line 20: "As soon as we covet . . ." From a conversation with Paul Bowler, a dear friend.

Believing the Guest

p. 155, title: "Believing the Guest . . ." This is the same
title of a poem of mine that appears in *Inhabiting Wonder*. In fact,
the epigraph is from the poem. What is at the center of this
poem has stayed with me, and I felt the need to explore it fur-

ther in prose. The two expressions are like buoys marking a deep, elusive theme.

There Is Something Else There

p. 160, line 8: ". . . north of the Capitol to the Soldier's Home . . ." In May 2005, I had the privilege of visiting the Lincoln Cottage in Washington, where I could feel the cross-hairs of the context that Lincoln faced daily. I am indebted to Erin Carlson, who works at the historical site, for bringing the interior Lincoln so alive. The details about Lincoln's summers at the Soldier's Home are taken from a fascinating book, *Lincoln's Sanctuary: Abraham Lincoln and the Soldier's Home*, Matthew Pinsker (New York: Oxford University Press, 2003).

Wholeheartedness

p. 165, line 16: "Courage is not abnormal . . ." From Jack Gilbert, "The Abnormal Is Not Courage" in *Monolithos* (New York: Alfred A. Knopf, 1962).

p. 166, line 1: "To live fully and willingly . . ." From Jane Hirshfield, "Facing the Lion: The Way of Shadow and Light in Some Twentieth Century Poems" in *Nine Gates: Entering the Mind of Poetry* (New York: HarperCollins, 1997), p. 163.

p. 166, line 10: ". . . be you perfect . . . Heaven . . . lead us not into temptation . . ." From *Prayers of the Cosmos: Meditations on the Aramaic Words of Jesus*, translated by Neil Douglas-Klotz (San Francisco: HarperSanFrancisco, 1990), pp. ix–x, 13–14, 17, 35.

p. 166, line 16: "*Tamim* was an Old Testament Hebrew word . . ." From Gail Godwin, *Heart: a Personal Journey through its Myths and Meanings* (New York: William Morrow, 2001), p. 35.

p. 167, line 8: ". . . the major traditions of the Middle East. . ." From *Prayers of the Cosmos,* p. 7.

p. 167, line 22: "The most significant teaching . . ." From Joseph Campbell, *Thou Art That: Transforming Religious Metaphor, edited* by Eugene Kennedy (Novato, CA: New World Library, 2001), p. xx.

p. 168, line 3: "Who sees all beings . . ." From *The Upanishads,* translated by Juan Mascaro (London: Penguin, 1965), p. 49.

Beginner's Heart

p. 169, epigraph: "I need to take a sacred pause . . ." From Dawna Markova, *I Will Not Die an Unlived Life* (Berkeley, CA: Conari Press, 2000).

p. 169, line 9: "In this way . . ." From a public conversation held with Archbishop Desmond Tutu at the Fetzer Institute, August 4, 2005.

Trust of This Kind

p. 172, epigraph: "To be invested with dignity . . ." From Abraham Joshua Heschel, *The Earth Is the Lord's: The Inner World of the Jew in Eastern Europe* (Woodstock, VT: Jewish Lights Publishing, 2001), p. 109.

p. 172, line 14: "To begin with . . ." Please see my discussion of how heart cells find a common beat in "The Fact of Our Oneness," in *The Exquisite Risk* (New York: Harmony Books, 2005), p. 78.

p. 174, line 22: "In conversation . . ." References to Bruce Carlson and his work arise from conversations I've been privileged to be a part of at the Fetzer Institute, where Dr. Carlson is one of our trustees.

Building on the Past

p. 179, line 21: "I became a historian . . ." From Howard Zinn, "Emma Goldman, Anarchism, and War Resistance," in *Artists in Times of War* (New York: Seven Stories Press, 2003), p. 39. This chapter is an edited version of a speech given by Howard Zinn at Radcliffe College, Cambridge, Massachusetts, January 29, 2002.

Tensions of Awakening

p. 186, line 7: "The Bodhisatta flew up into a Sal tree . . ." From Margo McLoughlin's translation from the original Pali of "The Wisdom of the Crows," in *Tell These Secrets: Tales of Generosity from Around the World*, edited by Ian Simmons and Margo McLoughlin (unpublished manuscript), p. 337. Many of these stories are available as a teaching resource at *www.LearningtoGive.org/materials/folktales.*

p. 187, line 26: ". . . emotional cowardice . . ." Menno Meyjes quoted in Jamie Melanowski's "Human, Yes, But No Less a Monster," *New York Times*, December 22, 2002, pp. 1, 36.

In the Middle of the Path

p. 198, epigraph: "To love everything . . ." Conveyed by my good friend George de Alth as he heard it spoken in an

Angeles Arrien workshop in which she quoted Rumi as saying that "Love is a flame that once kindled burns everything and only the journey and the Great Spirit remain."

Movement 3: Inner Courage and Where It Lives

The Interior Blessing

p. 202, line 20: "In October of 1944 . . ." From Dietrich Bonhoeffer, *Prison Poems*, edited and translated by Edwin Robertson (Grand Rapids, MI: Zondervan, 1999), pp. 19, 124–25.

The Secret Life of Detail

p. 205, epigraph: "Loving is the highest form . . ." For an insightful look into love as the highest form of knowing, see Parker J. Palmer, "Knowing is Loving," in *To Know as We are Known* (New York: HarperCollins, 1993), pp. 1–16.

p. 206, line 6: ". . . a deadeye . . ." Metal turnbuckles are now used to secure wires, called stays, which run from the top of the mast of a sailboat to the outer rails. These are used to stabilize the mast in high winds. But before turnbuckles, wooden blocks were used, and, because of the holes drilled for the stays, they were called deadeyes.

Our Fierce Impulse to Live

p. 210, line 12: ". . . from the work of Dr. Raymond Moody . . ." From a dialogue with Raymond Moody at the Fetzer Institute, May 31, 2006. Dr. Moody's research into the phenomenon of near-death experience had its start in the 1960s and led to his 1975 classic book on the subject, *Life After Life: The*

Investigation of a Phenomenon—Survival of Bodily Death (Nashville, TN: Guideposts Books, 1975).

The Work of Self-Return

p. 218, epigraph: "We are asleep . . ." From W. S. Merwin, *The Second Four Books of Poems: The Moving Target, The Lice, The Carrier of Ladders, Writings to an Unfinished Accompaniment* (Port Townsend, WA: Copper Canyon Press, 1992).

p. 218, line 4: "Children to Children . . ." Children to Children is a program in Tucson, Arizona, designed to help children deal with the grief of death. It was created in 1988 by Marianna Cacciatore, now the executive director of Bread for the Journey International, a nonprofit organization dedicated to nurturing the natural generosity of ordinary people. The story of Children to Children is in Marianna's unpublished manuscript, *Deep Presence: The Art of Being There for Someone in Grief.*

Burning the Raft

p. 221, epigraph: "Since the house is on fire . . ." From *The Sun*, October 2005, Issue 358), p. 48.

p. 221, line 11: " . . . his own teachings in this way . . ." In the *Diamond Sutra*, Buddha says, "You should know that all of the teachings I have given to you are a raft." *Sutra* in Sanskrit literally means *a rope or thread that holds things together*. In Buddhism, the term *Sutra* refers to a sacred scripture, one regarded as a record of the oral teachings of Buddha. According to tradition, a *Sutra* carries the actual words of the Buddha.

p. 222, line 20: "They heard it in Rumania . . ." The story comes from the Ashkenazi tradition which refers to the Jews, descended from Palestine, who first settled in Central and

Eastern Europe in the Middle Ages. *Ashkenaz* is the Hebrew word for *Germany*. The majority of Eastern European Jewry and their Ashkenazic culture was decimated by the Holocaust. For a soulful look into this world, please see *The Earth Is the Lord's: The Inner World of the Jew in Eastern Europe*, a small classic by the great Jewish philosopher Abraham Joshua Heschel (Woodstock, VT: Jewish Lights Publishing, 1995).

Giving Up What No Longer Works

p. 226, epigraph: "Sometimes snakes can't slough . . ." From *The Sun*, July 2005, Issue 355), p. 48.

p. 226, line 1: "Rabbi Alan Lew . . ." Rabbi Alan Lew is one of the leaders of the burgeoning Jewish meditation movement. His book *One God Clapping: The Spiritual Path of a Zen Rabbi* (Woodstock, VT: Jewish Lights Publishing, 2001), chronicles his years as a serious student of Zen Buddhism. His other books include *This Is Real and You Are Completely Unprepared* (Boston: Little, Brown, and Co., 2005) and *Be Still and Get Going* (Boston: Little, Brown and Co., 2005).

p. 226, line 8: "Saki Santorelli . . ." Saki, a dear friend, is author of *Heal Thy Self: Lessons on Mindfulness in Medicine* (New York: Harmony Books, 2000) and executive director of the Center for Mindfulness in Medicine, Healthcare, and Society at the University of Massachusetts Medical School.

p. 228, line 13: "In Psalm 46 . . ." From Gerald May, *The Dark Night of the Soul* (San Francisco: HarperSanFrancisco, 2005). Gerry passed away on April 8, 2005. He was a remarkable being whose clarity and passion touched all he came in contact with. He authored several important books, including *Addiction and Grace*. During his last winter, he shared with some of us what turned out to be his last manuscript, *The Power of The Slowing*, which was recently published posthumously as *The Wisdom of Wilderness* (San Francisco: HarperSanFrancisco, 2007). It is profound.

Judgment or Compassion

p. 232, line 11: "It is more important . . ." From Petrarch, "On His Own Ignorance and That of Many Others," quoted in Pierre Hadot, *What Is Ancient Philosophy?* (Cambridge, MA: Harvard University Press, 2002), p. xiii. Francesco Petrarch (1304–1374) was an Italian scholar, poet, and early humanist.

p. 232, line 23: "Mont Ventoux . . ." Mont Ventoux is by far the largest mountain in the region and has been called the "Giant of Provence." *Venteux* means *windy*, and indeed, at the summit, wind speeds as high as 180 mph have been recorded. The origins of the name trace back to the first or second century A.D., when it was named *Vintur* after the Gallic god of summits.

p. 234, line 5: "Even as a child . . ." From Doris Kearns Goodwin, "The True Lincoln," *Time Magazine*, July 4, 2005, pp. 48–54.

Experiments with Love

p. 236, epigraph: "All the arts we practice . . ." From the Web site *The Quotations Page*, *www.quotationspage.com*. M. C. Richards was a gifted and perceptive potter and poet who wrote the classic *Centering: In Pottery, Poetry, and the Person* (Middletown, CT: Wesleyan University Press, 1989).

The Gateway: Acceptance

p. 239, epigraph: "As soon as we accept . . ." From a letter cited in *Ahead of All Parting: The Selected Poetry and Prose* *of Rainer Maria Rilke,* translated by Stephen Mitchell (New York: Modern Library, 1995), p. 317.

p. 241, line 26: "... after thirty years, I knew that our bond had been cut ..." For a more detailed account of this relationship, see the earlier chapter, "Believing the Guest."

Sniffing Out What Is Sacred

p. 243, epigraph: "Sometimes a glance ..." From Llama Govinda, "The Way of White Clouds," in Jeff Humphries, *Reading Emptiness* (New York: SUNY Press, 1999), p. 4.

To Be a Clear Vessel

p. 246, epigraph: "Some day [we] will see ..." From *Roots and Wings: Poetry from Spain 1900–1975, a Bilingual Anthology,* edited by Hardie St. Martin (New York: Harper & Row, 1976), p. 3.

p. 249, line 1: "The word *Christ* itself comes from the Greek ..." For the history of anointing and of the evolution of the shaman's role, I am indebted to the invaluable contribution of Robert Noah Calvert for assembling *The History of Massage* (Rochester, VT: Healing Arts Press, 2002).

p. 249, line 14: "Tonglen embodies ..." From Andrew Weiss, *Beginning Mindfulness* (Novato, CA: New World Library, 2004).

Ways of Living

p. 252, line 5: "Wu Feng ..." Born in Amoy on mainland China, Wu Feng (1699–1769) grew up in Taiwan or Formosa. He served as an emissary and interpreter for the Manchurian government, living with the Ali or Tsou aboriginal Indians in the High Mountain region. The story of Wu Feng has been a teacher for me for many years. The opening passage here originally appeared as the April 28 entry in my spiritual daybook, *The Book of Awakening* (San Francisco: Red Wheel/Weiser and Conari, 2000), p. 140.

p. 253, line 9: "Richard Luttrell is a Vietnam Vet . . ." His story appeared on *Dateline* (May 1, 2000). A transcript of the *Dateline* piece is available from Burrelle's Information Services. Quotes here are from pp. 4 and 17 of that transcript.

The Beauty of It

p. 257, line 24: "The deepest thing I know . . ." Stanley Kunitz, *People Magazine*, date unknown. (This quotation, attributed only to a *People* interview, was cited numerous times in obituaries to Kunitz, who died in 2006. Of his many books, a good place to start might be *Passing Through* (New York: W. W. Norton and Co., 1997).

What Is Necessary

p. 267, epigraph: "I want to learn more and more . . ." From Friedrich Nietzsche, Book IV, section 276, of *The Gay Science: With a Prelude in Rhymes and an Appendix of Songs*, translated with commentary by Walter Kaufmann (New York: Vintage Books, 1974).

p. 268, line 7: "A living thing seeks . . ." From Friedrich Nietzsche, section 259, section 636, of *Beyond Good and Evil: Prelude to a Philosophy of the Future*, translated by Walter Kaufman (New York: Vintage Books, 1989).

p. 268, line 22: "God is dead . . ." This was initially written by Nietzsche in *The Gay Science*, first in section 108 ("New

Struggles"), then in section 125 ("The Madman"), and a third time in section 343 ("The Meaning of our Cheerfulness"). Note the progression of the subjects of the sections in which he revisits the idea. This by itself suggests a transformation. The phrase is also found in Nietzsche's classic work *Thus Spoke Zarathustra*, which is most responsible for its popularity.

p. 268, line 25: "God is dead. God remains dead . . ." (complete quote) From section 125 ("The Madman") of *The Gay Science*.

p. 269, line 15: "No longer being ashamed . . ." From Book III, section 275, of *The Gay Science*.

p. 270, line 9: "I want to learn more and more . . ." (complete quote) From Book IV, section 276, in *The Gay Science*. Termed by Nietzsche to be "the most personal of all my books," the second and more substantial edition of *The Gay Science* was published in 1887.

p. 270, line 28: "He never recovered . . ." Speculation continues as to the cause of Nietzsche's breakdown. His situation is frequently diagnosed as a syphilitic infection (http://en.wikipedia.org/wiki/Syphilis); however, some of Nietzsche's symptoms seem inconsistent with typical cases of syphilis. It is also conjectured that he suffered a form of brain cancer. Others suggest that Nietzsche experienced a mystical awakening, similar to those studied by Meher Baba. While many regard Nietzsche's breakdown as unrelated to his philosophy, some, including Georges Bataille and René Girard, argue that his breakdown was brought on by wrestling with his own philosophy.

Copyright Acknowledgments

About the Author

Mark Nepo is a poet and philosopher who has taught in the fields of poetry and spirituality for over thirty years. He has published twelve books and recorded three CDs. A new book of teaching stories, *As Far As the Heart Can See*, is forthcoming from HCI Books (Fall 2011). Recent titles are *Surviving Has Made Me Crazy* (CavanKerry Press, 2007), and *Inner Courage* (CD, Three Intentions, 2009). As a cancer survivor, Mark devotes his writing and teaching to the journey of inner transformation and the life of relationship.

In 2010, Mark sat down for an interview with Oprah Winfrey as part of her Soul Series on the satellite radio network, SIRIUS XM Radio. Of his books, *The Exquisite Risk* (Harmony Books) was cited by *Spirituality & Health* magazine as one of the Best Spiritual Books of 2005, calling it "one of the best books we've ever read on what it takes to live an authentic life." *The Book of Awakening* was a finalist for the 2000 Books for a Better Life Award and was cited by *Spirituality & Health* magazine as one of the Best Spiritual Books of 2000. Mark's collected essays appear in *Unlearning Back to God: Essays on Inwardness* (Khaniqahi Nimatullahi Publications, 2006). He is also the editor of *Deepening the American Dream: Reflections on the Inner Life and Spirit of Democracy* (Jossey-Bass, 2005). Other books of poetry include *Suite for the Living* (2004), *Inhabiting Wonder* (2004), *Acre of Light* (1994, also available as an audiotape from Parabola under the title *Inside the Miracle*, 1996), *Fire Without Witness* (1988), and *God, the Maker of the Bed, and the Painter* (1988).

His work has been translated into French, Portuguese, Japanese, and Danish. In leading spiritual retreats, in working with healing and medical communities, and in his teaching as a poet, Mark's work is widely accessible and used by many. He continues to offer readings, lectures, and retreats. Please visit Mark at: *www.MarkNepo.com* and *www.threeintentions.com*.

To Our Readers

Conari Press, an imprint of Red Wheel/Weiser, publishes books on topics ranging from spirituality, personal growth, and relationships to women's issues, parenting, and social issues. Our mission is to publish quality books that will make a difference in people's lives—how we feel about ourselves and how we relate to one another. We value integrity, compassion, and receptivity, both in the books we publish and in the way we do business.

Our readers are our most important resource, and we value your input, suggestions, and ideas about what you would like to see published. Please feel free to contact us, to request our latest book catalog, or to be added to our mailing list.

Conari Press
An imprint of Red Wheel/Weiser, LLC
665 Third Street, Suite 400
San Francisco, CA 94107
www.redwheelweiser.com